Letters from Belsen 1945

Letters from Belsen 1945

An Australian nurse's experiences with the survivors of war

MURIEL KNOX DOHERTY

EDITED BY JUDITH CORNELL AM AND R. LYNETTE RUSSELL AO

ALLEN & UNWIN

First published in 2000
Allen & Unwin
9 Atchison Street, St Leonards NSW 2065 Australia
Phone: (61 2) 8425 0100
Fax: (61 2) 9906 2218
Email: frontdesk@allen-unwin.com.au
Web: http://www.allen-unwin.com.au

National Library of Australia
Cataloguing-in-Publication entry:

Doherty, Muriel Knox.
Letters from Belsen 1945: an Australian nurse's experiences with the survivors of war.

Includes index.
ISBN 1 86508 222 8

1. Doherty, Muriel Knox—Correspondence. 2. Bergen-Belsen (Concentration camp). 3. World War, 1939–1945—Concentration camps—Liberation—Germany—Personal narratives, Australian. 4. Nurses—Australia—Correspondence. I. Cornell, J. A. (Judith A.). II. Russell, R. Lynette. III. Title.

940.53180943593

Set in 11.5/14pt MBembo by DOCUPRO, Sydney
Printed by South Wind Productions, Singapore

Cover design: Scooter Design
Cover photographs: National Archives (US), courtesy of USHMM Photo Archives (photo also reproduced on title page and chapter opening pages); photolibrary.com; Doherty Collection, New South Wales College of Nursing Archives, Sydney, DC/PB13

Foreword

MANY BOOKS, PAPERS, SEMINARS, courses and degrees have been devoted to an examination of the Holocaust and to the placement of survivors of the concentration camps. But what of those survivors who were not fit to be moved or who had no place to go? We have heard little of them.

Letters from Belsen 1945 fills that gap. We must be grateful to Muriel Knox Doherty for being a constant and remarkable correspondent, and for keeping copies—a not inconsiderable task in the days before word processors—and making them available to posterity. Her life was concerned with helping others and ensuring good nursing practices wherever she went. She always desired to be in the thick of things and so, in 1945, she joined the United Nations Relief and Rehabilitation Administration (UNRRA) and was appointed Chief Nurse and Principal Matron of the Bergen-Belsen Concentration Camp.

Miss Doherty had wonderful powers of observation and an ability to transfer them, as well as her difficulties and joys, onto paper. In her letters, she finds time to describe the conditions of Belsen on its liberation by the British. This is the only time that she gives a second-hand account but her description is riveting. No matter how often one hears or reads of the way people were treated in these camps, the horror does not lessen. She describes the difficulties of formulating a suitable diet for people who had been deprived of decent food—some for years—and people who were literally starving at the time of liberation. These accounts of the conditions before she arrived augment her own story and give us a picture of the utter desolation in which the survivors lived and died.

The job Miss Doherty took on seems insuperable. But she had proved throughout her life to be adept at solving apparently impossible problems. She was able to design a hospital, staffed by a polyglot population of nurses and patients. The patients, in varying degrees of ill health, were suffering from starvation, typhus and Tb among other things. The hospitals were ill equipped, without even sufficient blankets for the beds (partly explained by the appearance of people in grey flannel suits!). The DPs, even more, suffered from the hopelessness of their position. Miss Doherty attempted to make them feel as at home as possible and to do as much for them as she could. She had huge compassion and understanding for people who had been through hell and were having difficulty escaping from its memory and its effects.

She was deeply affected in particular by the plight of the Jewish survivors. Her description of the trials of the war criminals from Belsen and Auschwitz held in Luneberg is both compelling and horrifying. She attended the trials for only one day but the impression they left on her—and hence on the reader—could never be obliterated. She manages to convey her disgust at the enormity of what these people had done and leaves no doubt in the reader's mind of the arrogance and guilt of those accused.

Miss Doherty was a woman of selfless courage, wit and determination. She made an overcrowded hospital with very little equipment and personnel into a place where patients could recover their self respect, their traditions and their health. Her eyewitness accounts of her experiences at Belsen give the lie to those who attempt to deny that the Holocaust ever happened.

Cornell and Russell have done a great service by editing and publishing Miss Doherty's letters. Miss Doherty is so well able to show compassion, to convey her anger and disgust at the behaviour of the Nazis and others, and to describe with humour what must have been extremely difficult situations. It seems extraordinary to me that she ever found time to write her letters. But she was a woman who regarded everything she did as important. It seems to me likely that she needed to write her letters both to ensure that people would understand the situation and as an outlet for her feelings.

Anyone involved or interested in the Holocaust, in nursing, in courage and ability, will benefit by reading this book.

Vivianne de Vahl Davis BA PhD was a founding member of the Breast Cancer Action Group (NSW) and a Senior Lecturer in Communications at the University of Technology, Sydney, where she taught bioethics to nurses

These letters are dedicated to the countless millions who suffered and died in Europe— victims of the German New Order.

M. K. Doherty, Sydney, 1949

Contents

Editors' Note

This book brings together the complete collection of letters written by Muriel Knox Doherty to her friends and relatives during her time as the Chief Nurse and Principal Matron of the recently liberated Bergen-Belsen Concentration Camp. Some preliminary editorial work had been carried out on these letters by Miss Doherty following her return to Australia, when she was attempting to gain their publication. At this time she selected which of her letters she wished to be published and this selection has been respected by us.

In editing the letters, we have made every attempt to retain the flavour and style of Miss Doherty's writing. We have changed little, apart from standardising numbers and dates, correcting punctuation and the odd spelling mistake, or altering paragraphing. We have corrected grammar only where there was a glaring mistake or an obvious ambiguity in expression. Spelling that follows the conventions of the time has been retained throughout. Miss Doherty's original text contained many exclamation marks, double exclamation marks and underlined words—many of these have been deleted. Wherever possible we have listed at the beginning of the book the meanings of the abbreviations used by Miss Doherty throughout the text.

We have chosen to use the name 'Miss Doherty' throughout, instead of 'Muriel'—she would have found the use of her first name by anyone but close friends and relatives offensive. 'Miss Doherty' has therefore been used out of respect for this belief.

The supporting primary source material in this book has been selected from Miss Doherty's own collection which is now held in the Yad Vashem Archives, Holocaust Martyrs' and Heroes' Remembrance Authority, Jerusalem, Israel.

We are grateful to so many who have encouraged this publication: Judy Waters from JJ Editorial Services for putting us in touch with Elizabeth Weiss at Allen & Unwin, our publishers, to Meredith Rose and Colette Vella for their patience and editing talents, to Scooter Design for the wonderful cover and to the illustrator, Diane Booth, who so faithfully reproduced the hand-drawn maps.

We also extend our grateful thanks to the following people: Tony Cornell for all the assistance given during our time at the Yad Vashem Archives, where he willingly copied out pages of detailed material and gave advice and support; Dr Jaacov Lozowick, Director of the Yad Vashem Archives and his most helpful staff—in particular Judith Kleiman—for their assistance and permission to reproduce some of the material; and to the New South Wales College of Nursing, its Board (previously Council) and Executive Directors (Associate Professor Debora Picone and Professor Judy Lumby), for asking us to work on this manuscript and for supporting the visit to the Yad Vashem Archives.

R. Lynette Russell & Judith Cornell
Sydney, 1999

Abbreviations

AANS	Australian Army Nursing Service
ACC	Allied Control Commission
ANA	Australian National Airline
ATS	Army Territorial Service
BLA	British Liberation Army
BRCS	British Red Cross Society
CB	Companion of the Order of the Bath
CCS	Casualty Clearing Station
CIB	Central Intelligence Bureau
CO	Commanding Officer
DADOS	Deputy Assistant Director Ordnance Store
DGMS	Director-General of Medical Services
DMS	Director of Medical Services
DP(s)	Displaced Person(s)
MC	Military Cross
NAAFI	Navy, Army, and Air Force Institutes
OC	Officer Commanding
POW	Prisoner(s) of War
QAIMNS(R)	Queen Alexandra's Imperial Military Nursing Service (Reserve)
QM	Quartermaster
RAAF	Royal Australian Air Force
RAAFNS	Royal Australian Air Force Nursing Service
RAF	Royal Air Force (UK)
RAMC	Royal Army Medical Corps
RTO	Railway Transport Officer
SHAEF	Staff Head Quarters Allied Expeditionary Forces
SMO	Senior Medical Officer
Tb	Tuberculosis

UNRRA	United Nations Relief & Rehabilitation Administration
WAC	Women's Army Corps
WO1	Warrant Officer (1st class)

Preface

MANY PEOPLE HAVE ASKED me, during the war and since, how it was that I, an Australian nurse, came to be in the Nazi Horror Camp at Belsen. Even when I explained that I was there as Matron and not as victim, after the camp had been liberated and not during the German regime, these questioners seemed puzzled by the circumstances. Actually, there was no mystery about my appointment to Belsen, as the reader will learn, but much that was unusual and historic occurred during my term of service there. It is on that account that I venture to present the letters which I wrote while in Europe. They were not written for publication but to keep relatives and friends informed of my doings; they were written at odd times, in some very odd places, and often—particularly at Belsen—under very great difficulties, so I have thought it wise to tidy them a little. Many of the facts stated in my letters have since been confirmed by evidence given at the now famous Nuremberg Trials.

At the end of 1944, with the war in Europe drawing to a close and my work as Principal Matron of the Royal Australian Air Force Nursing Service slowing down to a series of local inspections and routine office duties (which my capable assistant could very well undertake), the plight of millions of displaced persons in the former occupied countries became increasingly compelling to me. The urge to help these people was so irresistible that I decided to apply for an appointment with the United Nations Relief and Rehabilitation Administration. Permission was granted by RAAF Headquarters and it appeared as if I would soon be doing a worthwhile job once more, as an administrative nurse with UNRRA in north-west Germany. Then delays, obscure in origin, postponed receipt of my discharge for many weeks. I waited with increasing exasperation but once release was given—at 6 pm on 23rd May—it was only thirty-six hours before I left Mascot Airport, Sydney, on my way towards the then unknown, but greatest, yet most tragic experience of my life.

Muriel Knox Doherty
Sydney, 1949

Chapter 1

BY AIR TO UNRRA

Muriel Knox Doherty in the uniform of the United Nations Relief and Rehabilitation Administration, London, 1945

(Temporary address)
20 Craven Hill
London W2
10th June 1945

The best way seems to be for me to commence my news from the early dawn on 25th May when Miss Michell—a welfare worker with UNRRA—and I emerged with our baggage from the ANA reception room at Mascot. The sky had opened up and the field appeared to be under water—our hopes of ever taking off were nil, or so we thought. However at 6.40 am off we went and soon found that the weather was only local. An attractive stewardess supplied barley sugar and the daily paper and repeated the former at intervals. It was no time before we arrived at Wagga—8 am—a frosty fresh morning. We only deposited some passengers and in ten minutes were on our way again. We had half an hour on the airfield at Narrandera and left at 9.15 am.

The fertile country around Mildura was in sharp contrast to the terrible country in the Riverina, as was the district approaching Adelaide, where we arrived at 1 pm Sydney time. Seven hundred and forty four miles in 4 hours, 50 minutes in a most comfortable Douglas. The clocks were put back half an hour, a performance which was necessary all along the route. Arriving at the ANA office in Adelaide I was pleasantly surprised to find Aunt Kit and Clarrie McLaughlin (Baker) awaiting me—however, there was much to do before we could eat. The WO1 had only been notified one hour before our arrival and their lunch hour was completely disorganised by finding us accommodation, which was eventually at the Hotel Richmond.

This was the beginning of what proved to be a non-stop canter from one authority to another, arranging tickets, weighing baggage, swearing to customs that we were not taking the Canberra Jewels out of Trust, etc, etc. We finally came to rest at a very nice restaurant and enjoyed a fish luncheon, after which Aunt Kit paraded me to her office staff at the *Advertiser* as, my niece who, etc, etc. However *she* was pleased and we then spent the afternoon at her flat and had dinner with the McLaughlins.

We took off from Parafield at 9.50 am, having been joined by Miss Butler, arrived at Ceduna at 10.40 am and departed 11.10 am to cross the 300 miles of the Great Sandy Desert to Forrest—what a desert, we could see the railway from time to time, but nothing else but arid wastes.

The trip to Perth from Adelaide is approximately 1400 miles and we did it in ten hours. Having written instructions to report to the Customs immediately on arrival, in spite of the fact that it was Saturday night and we knew not even a miracle would keep the officials on duty, we felt we must do so—and as I was officially in charge of the party, I felt that at least we should satisfy ourselves that they were not there, which we soon did! Accommodation had just been found for us at the Imperial Hotel and we just arrived in time to have a meal. Again three in a not too fresh room, however we were preparing for things to come. We were pretty tired by this time and were glad to have Sunday free.

We arrived at the Qantas office in Perth at 8 am. By this time Miss Butler had discovered that she had left her overcoat in the plane, which returned to Adelaide! Then the fuss began—that good lady, who has been in the AANS for five years, had come without a taxation clearance or cholera injection and we were due to leave Perth at 9.30 am—and planes wait for no man. I commenced ringing. First WO1, who was UNRRA's representative in Perth. He clearly told me he was not interested in us and could do nothing for us, then started a tirade about how overworked he was, etc. etc. I suggested he should notify UNRRA that he did not wish to undertake the work and I asked if he could suggest anyone who would help us with the Taxation clearance. Miss B rushed down to the Department, where fortunately she found the most helpful official, but had to produce someone to stand security for her—it was now 9.10 am. In the meantime I found the Chief Medical Officer at his home and he kindly offered to come in and give the cholera injection, which he did at 9.25 am. Qantas gave us a special car which finally deposited us at Guildford Airport—where by the way we found the overcoat!

The manoeuvres with the Customs, Security Officers, etc., and more weighing of baggage and self—by this time I scarcely know what my weight is, it has varied on so many scales! I put my sad tale to them about coupons and they helped me out, as you already know. After receiving a health clearance we had a welcome cup of tea and boarded our Liberator and took off at 11.40 am on the longest non-stop hop in the world. The trip from Perth to Learmouth on Exmonth Gulf was over terrible country, red dust and salt bush and the sun was blistering when we landed with one engine nearly on fire, (I believe). We again boarded our plane and took off at 5.15 pm and left Australia.

Thinking back over the long air trek—we travelled the Indian Ocean route—quaint recollections string themselves together, a necklace of memory. The amusing non-stop canters by our party of four at each port of call from one authority to another—form-filling, being weighed (with each set of scales produced a new figure!), and changing currency; the wear and tear of keeping name tags on one's luggage; and the morning over Ceylon when my ankles were so swollen that I was unable to put my shoes on until, frantic, I forced the bulging flesh inside just in time to join the mêlée round the Customs. The difference between anticipation and realisation in Colombo when we had so hoped for a warm bath and found instead a very dirty bedroom with the bedclothes of the last occupant still on the bed and his bathwater flooding the bathroom floor, the sewerage system having failed completely. At Karachi now, it was delightfully different. Even though we bumped over ruts to the city in a covered army wagon in blazing heat, when we arrived at the hotel there were snowy beds, mosquito nets, efficient room and laundry boys who responded to the touch of a bell so that our sojourn and our dinner at Karachi were blissful.

To Karachi we had already travelled by Liberator and RAF York planes in which the converted service seats felt rather like corrugated iron after a time. It reminded us that we were flying in a war-time transport and not a civil peace-time luxury airliner. However, the courteous attentions of the RAF Steward made up for any small discomfort.

Except on the York, our trek to the rear cabin for light refreshments in the form of sandwiches, fruit, coffee and lime juice (from enormous thermos containers) gave many opportunities for meeting our fellow passengers. Among these passengers there was an eminent English authority on food and nutrition, a member of an Indian Trade Delegation, a Professor from Palestine University, a British Diplomat and a number of RAAF personnel returning home on leave.

At Karachi we transferred to a Sunderland flying boat and headed for Cairo, via Bahrain where we ate roast goats' meat and cabbage in a wharf rest house with the thermometer showing 120°F! Looking down on the endless wastes of the Arabian Desert, where the only signs of life were some camel tracks and a few scattered nomad camps, we saw the Iraq to Haifa oil pipeline and the Great Rift, 3000 miles long from the Red Sea to Lake Tanganyika and the Sinai Peninsula,[1] over which the Israelites wandered for forty years, an area we cross in forty minutes! I remember flying over the main road through the desert to Alexandria and over remarkable sheets of salt water—green, magenta, maroon and purple, with thick white crusts at the periphery. Following the Mediterranean coast we skirted Tobruk where the Aussies made history and crossed to Sicily. As we circled over Augusta, with Mt Etna in the background, we were able to pick out many sunken planes and ships, remnants of the first Allied assault and landing. Our quarters in Augusta were in an Officers' Mess, formerly the Nazi Army barracks, the outer walls of which still carried slogans exhorting the Sicilians to victory.

It was Sunday in Augusta, and a feast day, so the population was out strolling in their best clothes, many with black mourning bands on their lapels. Front doors, too, had strips of black material tacked on them—grim reminders of recent fighting. Shrines and altars were set up in the street with fruit-salts bottles and empty shell cases holding candles and flowers.

Crossing the southern tip of Sardinia we flew across the French coast and up the Rhône Valley on the last lap of our journey. A great upsurge of affection for the Motherland began to stir within me. I remembered how, alone, she had stemmed the Nazi tide which threatened to engulf civilisation; how she had endured the blitz and how the voice of her grand Statesman, Winston Churchill, had brought hope and courage to not only those in the far outposts of our Empire, but to the unhappy peoples in the occupied countries of Europe. I was soon to see the illustrious scars wrought by her blood, sweat and tears—to talk with her people once more.

1 The Great Rift Valley actually runs from Jordan Valley in Syria to Mozambique.

I remember, how I remember, that first sight of England—the Swanage coast, clear, soft and lovely, and how I wondered when we landed at Poole if my Huguenot forebears had felt the same thrill as I, when they stepped ashore in England, even at this very spot.

Only an hour and ten minutes elapsed between our touch-down on the harbour and our departure from Bournemouth by train for London, a procedure that was an outstanding experience of English war-time efficiency. From the air during our eleven days (seventy-two flying hours) journey we had seen little evidence of war damage, but now as we drew near London we saw whole rows of workingmen's homes devastated, blocks of flats split open, hardly a roof undamaged. It was nearly seven in the evening when we steamed into Waterloo Station, some 12 000 miles from Sydney, and we were terribly tired. But there was one more effort with the luggage to be made, and another to appear not too unpleased that no accommodation had been booked for us. We made them both and were miraculously rewarded with generous hospitality at the American WAC's Club in Berkeley Square.

Next morning, after having reported at UNRRA Headquarters at 11 Portland Place, we began a strenuous round of meetings, lectures, instructions and preparations, and our non-stop canters entered their second edition as the various departments we had to find were scattered far and wide. Processing, as it was called, began on 5th June and had not ceased by 23rd June. Processing meant dealing with equipment, uniform, luggage, financial arrangements, insurance, allotments, coupon issue, inoculation, chest X-ray, passport clearances, travel vouchers, and many other matters which had to be finalised before our departure for the Continent.

Chapter 2

PROCESSING AND THE ROUTE TO BELSEN

Sketch of trucks taking prisoners into the forest by Muriel Doherty, Belsen, 1945

London
23rd June 1945

The first morning, after a cafeteria breakfast at the Club, we again packed up and moved to a guesthouse which UNRRA in the meantime had found for us. Three of our group share a large, bright, airy and comfortable room on the third floor. I'm rather like a mountain goat now, as lifts in London are still rationed for the lower floors and all are requested to walk down. At the moment we are in the throes of packing and are surrounded by camp beds, blankets, buckets, kitbags and valises, enamel plates, mugs and basins, jack knives, mess tins and K rations. All our books, papers, stamps and any printed matter which we wish to take to Europe have to be censored and heavily sealed before leaving. Even my diary, address book, calendar and directions for filling my pen!

London at first glance looks just the same as on my previous visit, it is only when one moves round and sees whole rows of terraces demolished and blocks of flats torn open that one realises what she endured. In some areas the damage is appalling but everything has been cleaned up so quickly and neatly that evidence of war is rapidly disappearing. A few days ago we came out of the Underground and were expecting to take our bearings from some heavy road blocks we had seen the previous morning, only to find they had completely vanished. Our quarters are not far from Paddington Station and this area has suffered badly, as have all the areas near the main rail arteries.

We took a very hurried bus trip to see St Paul's which stands proud and dignified among the ruins of the City—that business area of London which suffered so terribly in the 1940 blitz and fire, with eighty-eight nights of intense bombing without respite! Nelson still surveys Trafalgar Square from his Monument and the British lions appear disdainful and unharmed. I am anxiously wondering if I shall see the King and Queen and Mr Churchill before I leave and already have hovered round Buckingham Palace and No. 10 Downing Street in anticipation. The people of England are marvellous—cheerful, patient and most courteous everywhere, although some look very tired and wan. All, however, seem to be going about their work normally. The courtesy is outstanding as everyone queues up with no hurry, no pushing or jostling at all. The traffic is well regulated and the transport efficient, but not yet normal. It is almost impossible to buy a paper in the street because of the shortage of newsprint—all are reserved for regular customers. The other day we spied a hoary old newsvendor with his wares displayed along a low stone park-ledge. We enquired if he had any for sale and he obligingly rattled off the names of several. Explaining that we hardly knew one from the other, he hastened to enlighten us. 'There's the *Times*,' he said, 'them's fer the top notchers.' Passing along the row he paused, looked us up and down and said, 'Now, here's the *News of the World*, that's wot yer wants—they call it the barmaids Bible.' Feeling we were not exactly top notchers and guided by his choice, we gratefully purchased a copy and fled.

Everywhere one sees uniforms—Poles, Czechs, Norwegians, Free French, Dutch, Belgian—and one thinks of Warsaw, Lidice, Narvik and Arnhem. I believe the New Zealanders and Australians we see are nearly all ex-prisoners of war—they look fit and it is good to see the uniform. There seem to be quite a number of USA troops about and one frequently meets RAAF personnel. The British regiments represented are many and their colour patches and insignia interesting. There are foreigners everywhere, probably many are outcasts from their own countries, seeking sanctuary in this grand little island. The children I have seen, with a few exceptions, look extremely healthy, as they were given the correct food when adults went so short. Food *is* short, although there is plenty of carbohydrate because bread and potatoes are not rationed at present, but with very little meat, and fresh fruit and vegetables practically restricted to cabbage and greens (with carrots, lettuce and perhaps a slice of tomato occasionally), and sugar, milk and butter heavily rationed. It all becomes deadly monotonous and unappetising after a while. In a restaurant yesterday everything that I wanted was off—even the sausages (mostly bread) and mash. The waitress, wishing to be helpful, then brightly asked, 'Will you have a puddin'?' 'No thank you,' I replied, not wishing to commence with a sweet. 'No?' says she, raising her eyebrows in surprise and glancing at the next table. 'No puddin'!' she repeated, as if in doubt as to my sanity. Following her glance my eyes fell on a greyish, stodgy and moist-looking steak dumpling floating in some clear liquid and garnished with boiled potatoes and greens. Not wishing to shatter her faith in the culinary arts, I screwed up my courage and said I would try one, thinking as I did so of the shop I had seen in the Edgeware Road with a large yellow sign, 'Horsemeat: For human consumption only.' Nothing is wasted here—large bins labelled pig food, dry kitchen waste, rubber, paper, tins, bottles, and the like, invite the public to join in the drive for salvage.

In spite of its terrible hardships and deprivations London is just the same. The spirit of the place still lives and it is just that spirit which kept us Britishers free and on the map. One hears that their endurance was almost at breaking point when the V2 bombs were brought under control and the Allied invasion of Europe took place, but no one complains and I sometimes wish Australia could see for herself just what they have endured and how magnificently they responded to their ordeal. I spoke to a working woman—a typical Londoner—in a Lyons tea shop the other day. She told me that her husband was employed at John Lewis' in Oxford Street, and when they were bombed out of the shelter there they moved on to one at Selfridge's the same night and were bombed out again. Not once did she grumble during the whole conversation. 'Oh yes,' she said, 'managed with the food—just a bit of onion, some thyme and marjoram and a little egg powder added to the sausage meat, popped in a casserole with some nice brown gravy and there was a tasty dish when the ole man and me daughter come home in the evening.'

Soon after we arrived in London we were divided into groups, ours was No.15 in which there were about 150 people of all nationalities. The groups were then further divided into parties, with each group and party having their own leaders. Group 15 was to have moved to Paris and Granville (UNRRA training and mobilisation centre in Europe) early next week, but plans have been suspended owing to the Allied Control Commission taking over from SHAEF (Staff Head Quarters Allied Expeditionary Forces). The administrative positions which UNRRA had in mind for us were not ready and the Deputy Director General in UNRRA's Health Department, European Regional Office, suggested we might go out as Team Nurses pending development of our jobs. A team consisted of about thirteen men and women, each with a job to do. These teams organise and deal with displaced persons at Assembly Centres.

Without hesitation I said that I was prepared to go anywhere and do anything, as I considered it would all be experience and would help me to understand the work being done in the field. The nurse who was interviewed with me said she preferred to remain in London until her job was ready as she did not consider that the experience was necessary for us!

As it happened I did not go with a team; four days later the Deputy Director General told me that I had got top marks at my previous interview when I had said I did not mind what I did! He then told me he wanted me to go as Matron of Belsen ex-Nazi Concentration Camp Hospital, where I understand there are still some 10 000 patients. Little did I realise that an innocent remark would bring me what promises to be the most worthwhile job of my life.

FORM NO. F1-6 (18 JAN. '44)

UNITED NATIONS
RELIEF AND REHABILITATION
ADMINISTRATION

TRAVEL AUTHORIZATION

DATE 7th July, 1945.

TRAVELER Miss M.K. Doherty

TITLE Nurse

OFFICIAL STATION 21st Army Group H.Q.

UNIT D.P. Operations - Germany

THE PERSON NAMED HEREIN IS AUTHORIZED TO TRAVEL IN ACCORDANCE WITH THE REGULATIONS OF THE UNITED NATIONS RELIEF AND REHABILITATION ADMINISTRATION, SUBJECT TO THE CONDITIONS NOTED BELOW. THE DATE OF THIS AUTHORIZATION MUST APPEAR ON EACH EXPENSE ACCOUNT.

1. PURPOSE OF TRAVEL:

To take up assignment of matron at Belsen, Germany.

2. ITINERARY: FROM U.K. TO 21st Army Group H.Q. and thence to Belsen, Germany.

3. DURATION: BEGINNING ON OR ABOUT 7th July, 1945. ENDING ON OR ABOUT Upon arrival at Belsen, Germany.

4. PER DIEM IN LIEU OF SUBSISTENCE EXPENSES:

£

£ Living ~~or~~ field allowance in accordance with rates to be established in the area.

£ Actual subsistence expenses, not to exceed £1.15.0. per day, while in travel status.

£

5. OTHER CONDITIONS:

THIS SPACE FOR ACCOUNTING OFFICE

ESTIMATED COST:
TRANSPORTATION
PER DIEM
INCIDENTAL
TOTAL

ACCOUNT SYMBOL AND TITLE	NOTATIONS	AMOUNT

AUTHORIZED:

E.E. RHATIGAN,
Deputy Director General,
Department of Operations.
TITLE

APPROVED FOR CONFORMANCE WITH TRAVEL REGULATIONS:

FUNDS AVAILABLE:

UNRRA Travel Authorisation for Muriel Doherty to take up her assignment as Matron at Belsen, 1945

Visiting Officers' Mess
Main HQ
21 Army Group
British Liberation Army
10th July 1945

Our impatience at the delay in setting out was not improved when we found that the first signal from SHAEF requesting the Senior Medical Officer and myself at Belsen was sent on 23rd June with a second on 2nd July, and that neither seem to have been received by anyone at UNRRA HQ! All we knew was that we would be departing at any moment and, later, that the War Office was preparing fresh authority for us. So we began our final non-stop run to various UNRRA Offices, collecting passports, travel authorisations, Allied Expeditionary Forces' Permit for North West Europe, identity certificates, pay book, and last-minute papers to be censored and sealed. We have been told that we are only allowed to draw £5 per month on the Continent, and the remainder of my salary (less a number of deductions) therefore will remain in Australia.

Then the fun began. The War Office sent our fresh Movement Order by special messenger at 4.30 pm and which at 6 pm no one in any UNRRA Office had heard of. After much confusion and telephoning, the War Office finally decided to send a copy of the original, which was put into my hands at 6.30 pm.

After buying a thousand-franc note, as we expected to travel via France, I dashed back to our guest house in time for a last-minute bite of food before commencing the exhausting task of repacking. You see, previously we had been instructed to pack for a journey by road, and now we were told we could take only as much luggage as we could carry ourselves, as we were going by boat and train. I hopefully thought I could manage my kitbag, two large handbags, and a haversack, so readjusted that way, but by 11.30 pm, when the last article was stuffed in, I decided it would be impossible to take so much, and repacked once more. This meant a completely new inventory. Fortunately Dr Phyllis Tewsley, an Australian doctor with UNRRA, awaiting an assignment, nobly came to my rescue and typed the triplicate lists we were told to prepare and which to date have not been looked at, or even asked for, by one single official.

After three hours in bed, the borrowed alarm sounded and out I crawled, bleary-eyed and wondering why I was ever bitten by the UNRRA bug. Cook had a thermos of tea and sandwiches ready for me downstairs and my room-mate Helen Michell (another Australian) like a heroine went into the drizzling rain to Paddington Station in a vain search for a taxi.

We finally set out on foot, laden like pack-horses, to the Underground, en route to Fenchurch Station, away at the farthest end of London. I realised the kitbag would have been impossible under those circumstances and was so thankful I had decided to leave it to follow me. My escort did not arrive and so at Purfleet the Railway Transport Officer directed me to an Army lorry which drove me and my chattels to an Army Territorial Service Transit Camp where I was ushered into a Nissen hut of fifteen beds and given a welcome cup of very sweet tea. Healthy-looking German prisoners of war browsing in the warm sunshine and leisurely scything grass around the huts, whilst a British Tommy in charge read the latest *London Illustrated*, made me think of the contrast I was about to see at Belsen. I found I was to join a small party of Army and Red Cross nurses returning to Europe from leave, and that we were to move on that evening. A hot bath, offered as a special favour, I gladly accepted, not knowing when and where my next ablutions would take place. We were also issued with landing rations which consisted of a packet of twelve biscuits, two cakes of chocolate, two packets of cigarettes, a deflated life-belt, and three large, strong, lined brown paper-bags!

A tender took us to Tilbury where we stumbled over the gear of thousands of recumbent Tommies awaiting embarkation. Still no sign of my escort, but as I had spoken to him by phone earlier and found he had come by a later train, I did not worry. Then again to the censor and customs, etc. I exchanged £1 for 176 Belgian francs, and £1 for forty Allied marks, and was reprimanded for having the French currency which I had bought in London and too enthusiastically declared. Apparently there are a large number of counterfeits of the new currency in circulation and so they cross-examined me as to where I had procured mine.

Tubby Layton, as my Senior Medical Officer is affectionately known to his colleagues, and I travelled on separate troop ships. Mine, the *SS Mecklenberg*, was a smelly, exceedingly dirty Dutch transport, packed to capacity. There had been no time to clean these vessels during the war, and they looked tired and overworked. We women embarked first and so were able to watch the scene, including a final roundup of defaulters, from the deck. I was on active service at last, even though I had been considered too old for this in Australia at the outbreak of war.

On shore a huge fire blazed fiercely, and we were told that it was the store of the Imperial Paper Mills. The powerful jets of water directed on it had little effect and before we left the wharf a large area was gutted—and paper is so terribly scarce over here, too.

We dined on board at 10 pm—bare tables, bread and butter, tinned cheese, stewed chops, haricot beans and a mass of potatoes (the first really satisfying meal I had since arrival in England). After surreptitiously wiping out the enormous battered enamel mugs, we drank with relish the sweet, stewed, milky tea which had been mixed in the teapot.

All were issued later with rubber life-belts (we women already had ours) and red emergency lights. I smiled as I thought of the drill with our Mae Wests before leaving the Australian mainland. The instructor explained the use of the red light, whistle and automatic inflator, and advised us that we could always blow them up if the latter failed. My own vision of dog-paddling alone in the darkness of the Indian Ocean, wiggling my toes to keep the fish from nibbling whilst I puffed and blew, also came back to me, as did my relief when I found my seat in the *Liberator* was next to the rubber dinghies.

We retired to bed at 11 pm, and later the good ship *Mecklenberg* began to move to Southend. Sleep was impossible—troops paraded the deck over our heads all night and mysterious biters were very active also. The palliasse was hard, and as my pillow had been left behind in London I folded the ship's blankets, which were none too clean, and covered them with a calico bag meant for the palliasse and used this under my head.

Reveille was at 7 am and breakfast an hour later. It was a very calm night at sea as we moved through a minefield at five miles per hour with three sweepers ahead of us. The mines are magnetic, and I was told before sailing that they lie on the ocean bed and the vibration of the ship passing over them sets them off—nice thought! We were told also that they were set by the Germans to explode for 200 days—and that this time had not yet expired.

We circumvented a number of wrecks outside Ostend, which we sighted at 8 am, and at 10.30 am, still laden like a pack horse and joined by my SMO whose ship had arrived simultaneously in our convoy, I disembarked. The inevitable visit to the customs and embarkation offices then followed. After a cup of tea and cake at the Navy, Army, Air Force Institution we were conveyed in a fifteen-ton truck to our respective transit camps. Before we parted my escort decided, contrary to a very emphatic written instruction, that he would go direct to Bad Oeynhausen instead of to Brussels. Finally he was persuaded to send a signal to 21st Army Group, Monty's Headquarters, to say we were coming that way, as we had been notified that there would be no accommodation at Belsen unless we warned them in advance from Brussels.

Immediately on arrival at the Service Women's transit camp, I queued up for lunch and was surprised to find a one-time Royal Prince Alfred Hospital colleague, Fauna Campbell, in the same mess. She was proceeding to England for demobilisation from the Queen Alexandra's Imperial Military Nursing Service (Reserve) as her orders had come through since she last wrote from Belsen where her unit was posted. You can imagine how we talked! I wanted to hear so much at first hand about the patients I was to care for.

I prayed that there would be no through train to Bad Oeynhausen that afternoon, and was overjoyed to find that we were not to set out until the next morning.

We walked round Ostend in the heat, and saw what was left of the Atlantic Wall, which at one stage had so much publicity. Gigantic concrete gun emplacements, cleverly camouflaged to represent dwellings, were unrecognisable until we were almost upon them. The Belgians are gradually demolishing them but we could see the extensive damage to portions of them and to the surrounding houses and large hotels on the waterfront. The Belgian houses looked as neat as ever, with their fresh hand-made lace curtains and photos of King Leopold in many of the windows. The people who were taking their Sunday afternoon stroll were moderately well dressed and the children appeared fairly well nourished. Masses of people were sunbaking on the shady beach or browsing in the shade of gaily painted bathing boxes.

We had tea at the YWCA and tried to buy some fruit for the journey—but the price was very high and the quality very poor. Fauna looked tired. She has been through so very much and has had some extraordinary experiences. We talked far into the night and she gave me a graphic picture of what I would find at Belsen.

Another early morn departure with twenty-four-hour rations—sandwiches—and a truck drive over cobblestones to the station. A lovely morning—the fishing boats with their russet nets festooned from the masts made the harbour a picture. On the station were hundreds of baskets of their shimmering catch awaiting transport. We departed at 7.05 am, in a former German train which had very comfortable, upholstered plush seats.

Arriving at Bruges thirty-five minutes later, we saw the Belfry and Hôtel de Ville from the train and I thought of the hot potato chips I had eaten there fifteen years before! The surrounding country was neat and fertile, with quaint hayricks supported by a pole in the centre. An hour later we reached Ghent, where there was extensive damage round the station, with the rolling stock empty, rusting contorted skeletons. All the way to Antwerp there was evidence of recent war. Dumps of damaged planes, enormous tank parks and collections of wrecked vehicles soon became a familiar sight on all sides. Some of the houses picturesquely decorated with coloured tile fronts stood amid intense cultivation of crops, vegetables, clover, potatoes. Scarlet poppies, cornflowers and daisies thrived amid this devastation, almost screaming Mr Churchill's 'V for Victory' sign. We crossed many bombed bridges, replaced by newly constructed army structures, and at 12 pm entered Holland and saw the first windmill. Rosendaal was a badly damaged Dutch station but fortunately we were able to get some safe and cool drinking water from a fountain.

Quaint Dutch architecture with thatched roofs to the farm houses and coloured shutters, set in a background of rich fields and spruce forests, was in sharp contrast to the mass of twisted rails, burnt-out skeletons of whole trains, and the extensive damage seen round the railway marshalling yards. Fat cattle, beds of strawberries, raspberries, and asparagus surrounded bombed-out families living in tramcars and gaily painted caravans. The Dutch women were standing outside their homes to wave to the troop train. The children appeared poorly dressed. Everywhere there was evidence of thrift, with piles of twigs and branches of firewood all neatly packed in gardens amid huge round bushes of rose-pink and mauve hydrangeas and rounded thatches on the centre poles of the hayricks. Each farm seemed to have one draught horse and about five or six head of cattle, a couple of pigs, a sheep or two, a few goats, fowls, and an orchard.

About 3 pm we crossed the River Meuse where the original bridge could be seen lying in pieces in the river, suggesting that it had been demolished by the retreating Germans. Our train crawled over the temporary structure on a single track and arrived at Gennep, where a long flower-bedecked train, covered with French slogans, '*Vive de Gaulle*' and '*Vive la France*', stood. It was packed with French refugees, men and women, who were strangely quiet and who were being repatriated from Germany and Austria.

Another truck drive to a British transit camp, tented and cool. Being the only woman on the train I was to have the place of honour on the seat beside the driver. Alas! My skirt was extremely narrow and short (wartime restrictions) so great difficulty was experienced in gaining a foothold on the axle.

Whilst a helpful British Tommy gave a mighty heave from behind, I came to my knees on top of the five-feet-high wheel and subsequently fell clumsily into the cabin. The driver explained that he *nein sprechen English*, and I that I *nein sprechen Dutch*, but nevertheless we carried on quite a friendly conversation.

We drove through the town and circumnavigated masses of tangled wires. Not one house or building was undamaged (a land mine had scored a direct hit).

At 5.30 pm we entered British Occupied Germany, or the British Zone as it is called, at Phalzdorp—where there was extensive damage to the few visible houses. Our train was the first to pass on this line since it had been repaired.

At Cleve the devastation was terrific, huge sections of rails and sleepers evulsed [sic] across the road, and enormous torn camouflage nets spread over damaged gasometers. German women were searching for loot among the ruins, loading prams and barrows.

We crossed the Rhine that evening by a narrow, improvised bridge, somewhere in the vicinity of the first British crossing at

Wesel, I think. A town nearby was in complete and absolute ruins, and rows and rows of what had once been trains were now one tangled mass of steel. Large areas were wired off and interlaced with white material, with a notice. 'Mined', attached. I remembered Goering's famous boast: 'and not one single bomb will fall on Germany'.

The children look healthy, and the crops everywhere are in abundance at present—the result of slave labour, of course. There was also more cattle here than on the Dutch farms. We are told that the Germans stole them from the Dutch, and that as soon as possible after the cessation of hostilities the Dutch crossed the border and took back all that they could find!

General Montgomery recently issued an order that the British soldiers might fraternise with German children under ten. There was an obviously organised galaxy of waving on the part of every German child in the district as we passed. It was, of course, as I mentioned, the first British train that had come through as far as Bad Oeynhausen, and so was an event in itself. It was light until quite late, being double summer time and twilight. We passed a pile of RAF plane wreckage, which brought to mind the British Broadcasting Commission voice we knew so well: 'some of our planes did not return'.

At 9.10 pm we came to Coesfeld and no words could possibly describe the utter devastation. It had probably been an important German marshalling yard, and if you can imagine one of our own with all the engines as far as you can see, blasted and overturned; lines and lines of trucks and carriages in the same condition; miles of rails and sleepers ripped up, twisted and balancing grotesquely like gaunt skeletons; and all buildings in the vicinity in complete ruins, you will have some idea of the scene. Bomb craters everywhere. All this set in a background of intensely cultivated country makes you wonder why Germany ever started the war, and laid herself open to pulverisation such as this. Of course a good deal of the damage was probably done by her own retreating armies. The number of churches still standing is in marked contrast to the hundreds in England in complete ruins or gutted by fire.

At 10 pm we came to what was once Rheine, and witnessed an even more chaotic scene. The bridge across the river had either been demolished by the Germans or destroyed by the Allies.

Festoons of twisted rails draped the embankment. There was evidence of local fighting here also, as well as enormous bomb craters. It was now thirteen hours since we entered the train, and I was feeling, and probably looking, decidedly grubby after handling the greasy sausage rolls and sandwiches from our rations. At Osnabrück we were handed most welcome mugs of sweetened tea, ladelled from a dixie by a cheerful British Tommy, and another bag of sandwiches!

Here we had one and a half hours' halt, but as it was dark could only exercise on the platform. At 2.30 am we arrived at Bad Oeynhausen, were met by the RTO and directed to the Visiting Officer's Mess at the Victoria Hotel, where after a quick wash I thankfully fell into a large feather bed and covered myself with a soft, cerise German eiderdown and slept.

There is a notice in the entrance hall which reads in English, 'This hotel, reserved for officers of the rank of Colonel and above and equivalent ranks in other services and allied forces, and certain important civilian visitors who are visiting H.Q. on official business only.' We are not sure into which category we fall, but we like to imagine the latter—particularly as we were asked to sign the visitors' book, which contained such illustrious names as Monty's!

A cheerful Fräulien brought me a cup of the usual brand of tea in the morning, and after a welcome bath and a good breakfast, my SMO and I reported to 21st Army Group Headquarters, and there met various officials, medical and otherwise, who were interested in us. An outline of the early and terrible days when the British liberated Belsen Camp was given to us. We then drove some fifty miles to Herford where we met the Director of Medical Services 21st Army Group, and Senior Principal Matron QAIMNS, after which we bumped over the cobbled streets at 55 mph!

British Army personnel everywhere, and things generally appear to be returning to normal. Civil affairs are in the hands of the German burgomaster and the local authorities. German officials are on stations and directing some of the traffic. The barracks we visited had recently been a Nazi stronghold and an arrogant eagle surmounting a swastika was carved on the wall. All signs, of course, of the Nazi regime had to be removed when the Allies occupied the country, but there are so many that it will take some time to eliminate them. It was good to see the Union Jack fluttering above all.

The district was rich in crops from roadside to horizon, some crops five to six feet high. We passed a convoy of the first batch of ex-Wehrmacht farmers, returning to the land to bring them in. All wore yellow triangles, denoting demobilisation, and looked shabby, sullen and unkempt. After a short rest in the afternoon we walked in some lovely gardens and watched a fountain (shot with rainbow colours) playing.

F. Tannenbaum, 'Life in Concentration Camp' series, Belsen, 1945

Visiting Officer's Mess
Main HQ
21st Army Group
British Liberation Army
11th July 1945

We have spent the last twenty-four hours since our arrival in Germany at the above mess, and after calling on the UNRRA representatives in Bad Oeynhausen and paying my account of six marks (3/-), the UNRRA Medical Administrator of Belsen Camp, my SMO, and I are awaiting transport to Belsen in half an hour.

We are to travel in a jeep with Dr W. A. Davis, USA Medical Corps (Consultant in Typhus attached to 21st Army Group from the USA Typhus Commission), who directed and controlled anti-typhus measures at Belsen camp on liberation. I have been told that Dr Davis' work and that of the British field Hygiene Section undoubtedly resulted in preventing a widespread epidemic of typhus in Europe. Dr Davis has warned us that he always drives just as fast as he considers safe, so you can imagine my feelings! If I survive and am in a fit condition, you will receive this letter completed.

Later

Well, whether I am in a fit condition is a matter for conjecture, but here I am! At 9.45 this morning I packed myself between the luggage in the back of the jeep (my SMO preferred the front seat) and prepared for the worst. We travelled between fifty and fifty-five miles per hour on roads of all kinds—some moderately good, others cobbled and many rich in craters. Had I not watched for the bumps ahead, grasped the handle of the suitcase on one side and my haversack on the other and raised my hinderparts from the saddle, as it were, there would have been multiple fractures of the spine and pelvis, I'm sure, for our speed did not slacken for a small thing like a bomb crater.

Although summer, the lashing wind cut my face and wrought havoc with my hair, which was most devastating, for we were to call on HQ of 30th Army Corps (under whose authority the

UNRRA Operational Unit at Belsen was to function) and I did want to look tidy.

We followed rivers and canals some of the way in a very picturesque countryside. There was more evidence of street fighting as well as aerial bombing. We passed burnt-out woods where flame throwers had attacked pockets of troops, and crossed several newly constructed army bridges. It was good to see British troops in occupation and street signs in English as well as German.

We arrived at our HQ at Nienburg about noon, and saw dozens of overturned tanks, cars, and anti-aircraft guns all burnt out, and piles and piles of unused ammunition. Farm houses appeared prosperous, built mainly of red brick, half timbered, with a large barn adjacent or nearby. We passed innumerable lorries, farm carts, push carts, wheelbarrows, buggies, and old-fashioned carriages laden with the luggage and household goods of German evacuees returning. A small white cross surmounted by a British steel helmet alongside a roadside studded with fox-holes was a grim reminder of the fierce battles which had so recently been fought there.

We met all the HQ Staff Officers and lunched at their mess, and later collected our passes—mine permitting me to enter Belsen Camp to take up the post of Head Nurse to the Senior Medical Officer. As we left we ran into heavy rain, but we put up the hood and kept the worst of it out as we skidded along the road. The country had changed from rich farm-lands to lovely wooded areas and it was hard to believe that it could have concealed such horrors, as there is ample proof it did. We passed the peaceful and picturesque little village of Bergen-Belsen and saw the long military railway platforms and the road winding down to that small clearing in the forest now known to the world as the Horror Camp.

I visualised those last terrible months of the war when the decisive battles were raging. The Nazis, knowing they were losing, endeavoured to hide the evidence of their wholesale brutality. They feverishly transported thousands of slave workers from Bremen, Hamburg and other areas to Belsen in open trucks and on foot, in the depth of winter. The concentration camp was already grossly overcrowded and rotting. These miserable people were driven into the nearby forest when there was no more space in the camp. Epidemics were raging, thousands were dying without medical aid. When the forest was full and the disintegration of the Nazi regime had set in, the victims were left in open trucks at this village railway station, among the dead and dying, without shelter, food or water. Death was a merciful release. The villagers must have known what was going on, but I am told that when the British ordered the German civilians and members of the Wehrmacht to visit the camp and view the result of Nazi *Kultur*, many denied having known what was taking place.

In my letters I shall endeavour to tell you how some of these victims of the Nazi terror found freedom after having suffered the tortures and terrors of the ghetto and the concentration camp.

It was about 5 pm when we drove into the camp and I suddenly realised with tremendous force that what I was about to see was all a deliberate part of the awful suffering, the unbelievable tragedy and the colossal disruption which the Nazi-Fascist scheme for world domination had attempted to impose on humanity.

As we were unexpected officially (the signal notifying our arrival came through the next day!), temporary accommodation had to be arranged. While waiting, Major Davis drove us round the present camp, a former German Army Barracks, to which the British authorities had evacuated the survivors of the Horror Camp, to give us a picture of the whole area. Some roads must be about three miles long—I shall describe it in detail later. We passed many so-called fit people wandering round in the rain, little children playing in the puddles and saw great activity round the cook-houses. How I was aching to get into the thick of it all!

The Officer in Charge, Military Government, was rushing to a conference, so I talked to a pretty Czech Jewess, Brunehilde, who was working in the office. Being young and intelligent, she told me, she was forced to work for the Germans in Ruthenia and later in Hungary. She was thrown into Belsen two days before liberation. Her entire family—her parents, her sister and the sister's two children, and all her aunts and cousins—were all exterminated in the Nazi gas chamber and crematoria at Auschwitz in Poland.

She explained how on arrival at the extermination camp, she and other prisoners were stripped naked and marched before the SS Guards—mainly men. The usual selection took place, when the so-called fit and young were marched one way and those of no use to Germany or the Germans were marched in the other direction. The latter were told they were going to the bath, and were never seen again. She said people were sometimes insufficiently gassed before cremation, with children not always being gassed first. Brunehilde had recovered from her illness sufficiently to work in the Administration Office here.

I also met a young Rumanian Jew, a technical engineer from Paris University. He had been a POW and was marched by the Germans with hundreds of others, barefoot, from Eastern Europe to Belsen during the Russian advance. Although exhausted and ill on arrival he had recovered fairly well, and is now acting as a guard for the British.

The Commanding Officer invited us to be his guests until accommodation could be found for us, and after collecting two army blankets and a pillow case each, we were driven to a comfortable German farmhouse at Dageford village, some fifteen minutes from the camp, where he and several of his Senior Officers live.

CHAPTER 3

THE LIBERATION

Belsen in the hour of liberation

C/- 168 Military Government Detachment
British Liberation Army
Belsen
16th July 1945

The SMO and I anticipated that we would be taking over the hospital from the British Army authorities very soon after our arrival. Now we find that no arrangements for the early arrival of our medical and nursing staff seem to have been made by the UNRRA HQ in the British Zone. Nor is there any accommodation available here for the number we shall require to replace the present army staff. We have not even a room in which to work when at the hospital. The British CO and Matron have put their offices at our disposal and are doing all they can for us, but it is disgusting to think that, first we had the unnecessary delay in departure from London and now we cannot even tell them when we will be able to take charge. Although our time is already fully occupied with preliminary arrangements, it is all rather embarrassing and a reflection on the Administration.

In the meantime I shall try to tell you what I have gathered of the liberation of Belsen concentration camp by the British, from Dr Davis and from personnel who were working here at the time, from patients, Army Authorities and official documents.

The Battle of Minden had been won. Allied soldiers were deployed in the surrounding districts. Decisive battles of the war were being fought all round the Belsen area, when on 12th April 1945 two members of the Wehrmacht approached the advancing British with a white flag. They stated that in the neighbouring country there was a camp where Allied prisoners had been without food for six days and that they, the guards, were unable to get any supplies or water—actually it was later revealed that the prisoners had been deliberately starved for a considerable time and kept without food and water during the last week.

The Chief of Staff of the First German Para Army approached the Brigadier General Staff of the British 8th Corps. He explained that typhus was raging in the camp and invited the British to take it over to prevent the epidemic spreading over Europe. He asked that a special three-day truce be arranged. This was agreed to.

On 13th April the terms of the special truce were drawn up. The British agreed to take over the camp (which was to be handed over intact), including all official records of the inmates. The German SS were to remain and the Hungarian regiment of about four thousand men, which had been brought in by the Germans before liberation to reinforce the SS, were to remain also and be used by the British as they wished.

As bitter fighting was going on all round, few British Army Medical and Nursing personnel could be released before the capitulation of Germany, but an SOS was sent to British HQ for assistance. Brigadier Hugh Llewellyn Glyn Hughes, Deputy Director of Medical Services, 2nd Army, is believed to have been the first to arrive in the camp.

The infamous Belsen Concentration Camp was liberated by a British Unit (about 240 men), an anti-tank battery of the 63rd anti-tank regiment, which arrived on 15th April. This unit brought some glimmer of hope and life to those who had despaired of ever being free again.

A loud speaker was taken into the camp and a British intelligence corps officer, Captain Derek A. Sington, announced that the British were taking over. I believe that in the women's camp the sound of weeping and hysterical laughter was so loud that this announcement was almost inaudible.

The same afternoon the British brought in twenty-seven water carts, and food for all, for the evening meal was provided. It is said that the psychological effect of this was amazing, although there were thousands who unfortunately were too ill to benefit.

The Royal Army Medical Corps under the command of Lt Colonel J. A. D. Johnstone, Officer commanding the 32nd British Casualty Clearing Station (and later SMO of Belsen Camp), the 11th Light Field Ambulance and two Hygiene Sections began work on 17th April. With the Casualty Clearing Station were eight Sisters of the Queen Alexandra's Imperial Military Nursing Service—the first women to arrive at the camp.

Lt Col Mather with the 113th Light Anti-tank Regiment, HQ 10 Garrison and 224 Military Government Detachment entered the camp on 18th April. The first British Red Cross and St John's

Ambulance teams, with four Sisters, arrived on 21st April and from that date a steady flood of reinforcements from British and international voluntary organisations into the camp began.

Fauna Campbell, who you will remember was previously on the staff of the Royal Prince Alfred Hospital, Sydney, and who served with the QAIMNS(R) during World War II, arrived at Belsen with the advance party of the 9th British General Hospital on Sunday 29th April. The American Field Service, a voluntary body attached to the British Army, transported this group from Holland to Belsen and remained some weeks assisting with the evacuation of the Horror Camp. The remainder of the 9th BG Hospital, arrived on 3rd May. The unit at first assisted the 32nd CCS and on 7th May opened their own hospital in another portion of the barracks, where they had beds for 4000 patients.

Imagine a desolate clearing in the forest, entirely cut off from the outside world, about three miles from the little insignificant village of Bergen-Belsen and eighteen miles from the nearest town. There are about one hundred ramshackle wooden huts on either side of the main pathway, and administrative buildings one end and the crematorium and graves at the other. There are also five cook-houses and masses of barbed wire everywhere. This will give you some idea of the site of Belsen Concentration Camp No. 1.

The camp, under the Germans, actually consisted of two sections—Camp No. 1, the Horror Camp, situated in a small clearing in the forest, which on liberation contained approximately 40 000 desperately ill and starving men, women and children. A section of the huge modern German Panzer Training Barracks, or *lager,* less than one mile away had been recently taken over by the Germans for an overflow of some 16 000 men and was known as Camp No. 2. These men had been driven from other concentration camps in Europe by forced marches and had only been there a few weeks. They were free from typhus, although suffering from starvation.

Between the two camps, hundreds of men, women and children destined for Camp No. 1, but for whom there was no room, had been forced to live in the open, under the trees, with insufficient food and water and no shelter or warmth. All were closely guarded by the ruthless SS men and women, who shot them if they attempted to escape.

The actual area in which the 40 000 prisoners were confined in Camp No. 1 was approximately eight miles long by four miles wide, enclosed by heavy barbed wire fences (possibly electrified). This area included a large section for the German administration blocks and another for the crematorium and accessories.

I am enclosing a plan which I copied hurriedly from one drawn by the British officials and which was lent to me for this purpose. You will see there are fourteen observation towers, whose powerful searchlights pierced the intense darkness of the camp at night. [See page 41.]

The huts, each about 30 × 10 yards with no furnishings whatsoever and built to hold from thirty to fifty persons, are stated at one time to have held up to 1000 and contained anything up to 600 when the British came. The inmates were virtually imprisoned within them, for those who dared to emerge in search of food or water were all most certainly shot by the SS guards or the Hungarians.

On the day on which Joseph Kramer, the SS Commandant of Belsen, was being interviewed by the British Military officials, I believe the SS guards were actually shooting starving prisoners who were trying to take some raw potatoes from the cook-house. Kramer made no attempt to stop his men until he was told that one SS man would be shot for every internee shot. Even then the Germans made no attempt to help the wounded and dying.

By the way, we hear that Kramer and those of his henchmen who survived are now in a nearby prison awaiting their trial, and we are told that the Wehrmacht stoned him when he was being transported to the aerodrome to his trial. One SS man hanged himself and several others committed suicide by trying to escape. Those who attempted to escape were shot by our men, as they knew they would be, but evidently preferred this to burying the dead, which was the task allotted to them by the British.

Within a stone's throw of the unutterable squalor and filth of the concentration camp where the unfortunate victims of the Nazi regime were imprisoned were the magnificent quarters provided for units of the German Army. These Panzer barracks, situated in lovely surroundings, cover an area in the forest of about three to four miles. A heavy barbed wire topped fence encloses this area with four entrances, to the North, South, East and West, complete with guard rooms and sentry boxes. The roads inside are in fair order and lined on either side with lawns, trees and shrubs. There are over one hundred large two-storeyed stucco concrete blocks of buildings with cellars and attics, each built to accommodate 150–200 German Army men. All are fitted with sewerage systems and heating stoves. In addition to the buildings used for living accommodation are the HQ and other administrative buildings, quartermasters and ordnance stores, workshops, canteens, cook-houses, lecture halls and libraries. Near the centre of this camp is a modern concrete cinema and concert hall, complete with upholstered seats and private boxes which no doubt were reserved for the upper crust of the Nazi regime. Further away is a very large tented air-conditioned theatre, built with metal supports rather like a giant meccano. It would probably accommodate three or four thousand or more. Stables and parks for cars, bicycles, heavy military vehicles and tanks are plentiful. There was also a large shimmering blue swimming pool and modern tiles, steam-heated bath and shower rooms, providing the essence of comfort for the German Wehrmacht.

Groups of four and five buildings are arranged round a concrete square or parade ground where many goose-stepping, heel clicking, Heil Hitler demonstrations probably took place. The whole barracks area is now divided for convenience into Camps 2, 3 and 4. The palatial circular German Officers Club—called by the British the Round House—with its magnificent ball-room, banqueting hall, solarium and ante-rooms, crystal chandeliers, parquet floors, and swimming pool stands in a lovely secluded wooded area of these vast barracks. On the lower ground floor are vast kitchens fitted with the latest stainless-steel labour saving equipment, capable of catering for very large numbers.

On liberation the barrack store-rooms contained enormous supplies of food, including 600 tons of potatoes, 120 tons of tinned meat, and large quantities of flour and medical supplies, etc. The camp bakery had a daily capacity of 60 000 loaves. There is also a large steam laundry in the vicinity.

A rustic bridge crosses a lake on which one white swan reigns supreme. Nearby among the trees is an attractive half-timbered house, now used by the British as a Military Officers' mess. It is well furnished and fitted with every convenience, including a large refrigerator in the basement. It was in this refrigerator that Kramer, the Beast of Belsen, is said to have been locked when captured and awaiting removal to prison! In a lovely spot nearby, among oaks, elms, maples and beeches, is the large square white residence of the Commandant of the Panzer training school, who is now in prison also, although his wife is still said to be living there.

Outside the main gates of Camp 3, and in the surrounding area, are numbers of solidly built two-storeyed blocks of flats, probably used by the German Army as married quarters for their personnel. Overgrown vegetable gardens and orchards surround many. Double windows, with outside thermometers attached, cumbersome bath heaters, modern electric stoves and a variety of heavy furniture, cooking utensils and delicate china and glassware are indicative of very comfortable quarters.

Prosperous German farms with fat cattle, horses, pigs, geese, ducks, hens and rich crops abound in this area. I should say the standard of nutrition among the Germans around here, especially the children, was quite high.

About half a mile outside the barracks area in a spruce forest is a large, 250-bed modern brick Lazaret—the German Military Hospital serving the Panzer Training School and now known as the Glyn Hughes Hospital. In this area there are five main blocks with wings branching off, surrounding a central lawn and gardens. The wards are built to accommodate from one to fourteen persons. The fittings are modern, with wide corridors, very wide, and utility rooms which are plentiful and convenient. All the wards are equipped with modern hospital bedsteads and good mattresses.

A number of the ground-floor wards open onto verandahs and a terrace facing the sports ground, as well as onto the front lawn. Attractive shrubs grow closely round the outside walls. Beneath the clock tower, carved in stone, is a huge swastika surmounted by a German eagle, the symbol of the Nazi Party.

A modern operating theatre, with spacious sterilising, anaesthetic and utility rooms, is situated at one end of the administrative block. There are well-equipped kitchens, store-rooms, mattress disinfectors, post-mortem rooms, and garages. A continuous underground cellar—probably used as an air-raid shelter for the Panzer staff—extends practically the whole length of the buildings and the attics are spacious, though unlined. The hospital is fitted with steam-heating apparatus and provided with double-glazed windows.

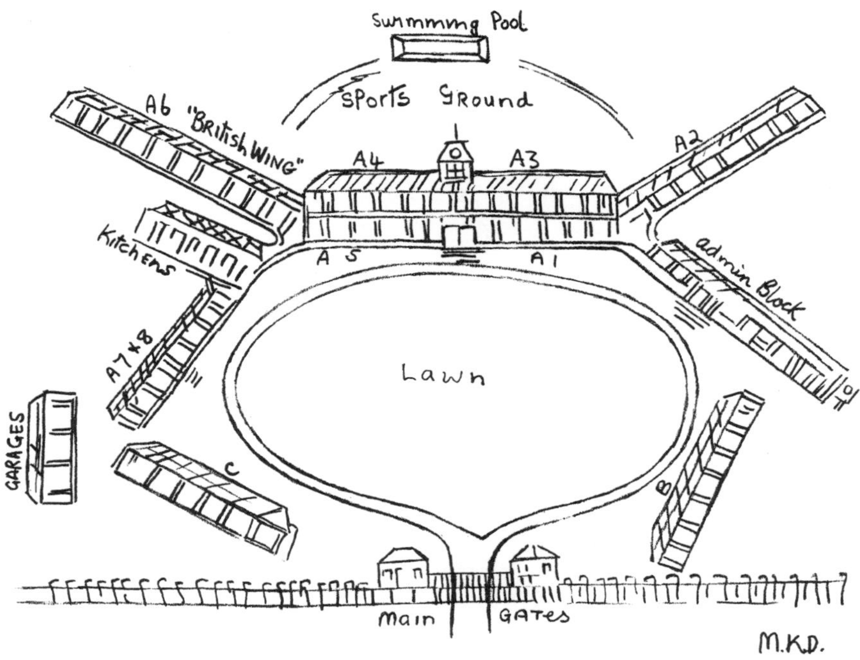

Rough plan of Glyn Hughes Hospital, Belsen, 1945

The Officers' wing is particularly well furnished, with attractive figured-linen window curtains, heavy plush arm chairs, and an extraordinary number of scarlet-and-green painted wooden flower-pot stands of various designs. The German army certainly surrounded itself with every comfort in this barracks!

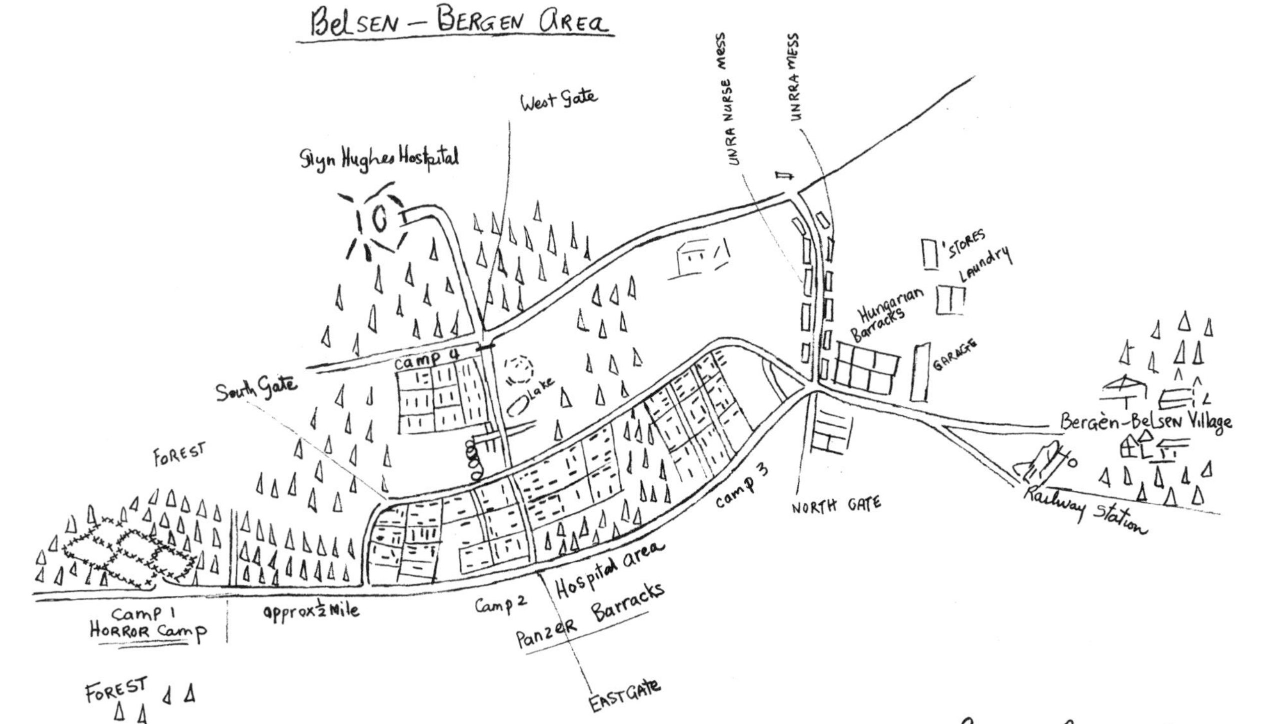
Belsen – Bergen Area
West Gate
UNRRA Nurse Mess
UNRRA Mess
Glyn Hughes Hospital
Stores
Laundry
Hungarian Barracks
Garage
Camp 4
Lake
South Gate
Bergèn-Belsen Village
Forest
Railway Station
Camp 3
North Gate
Hospital area
Camp 2
Panzer Barracks
Camp 1
Horror Camp
approx ½ Mile
Forest
East Gate
Rough Plan of Camp No1 "Horror Camp" and Camps 2, 3, 4 in Panzer Barracks
Camp no1. about 2 Kilometres away from Panzer barracks, hidden among pines & surrounded by wire – about 15 miles north of Celle

Sketch map of the Bergen-Belsen area, 1945

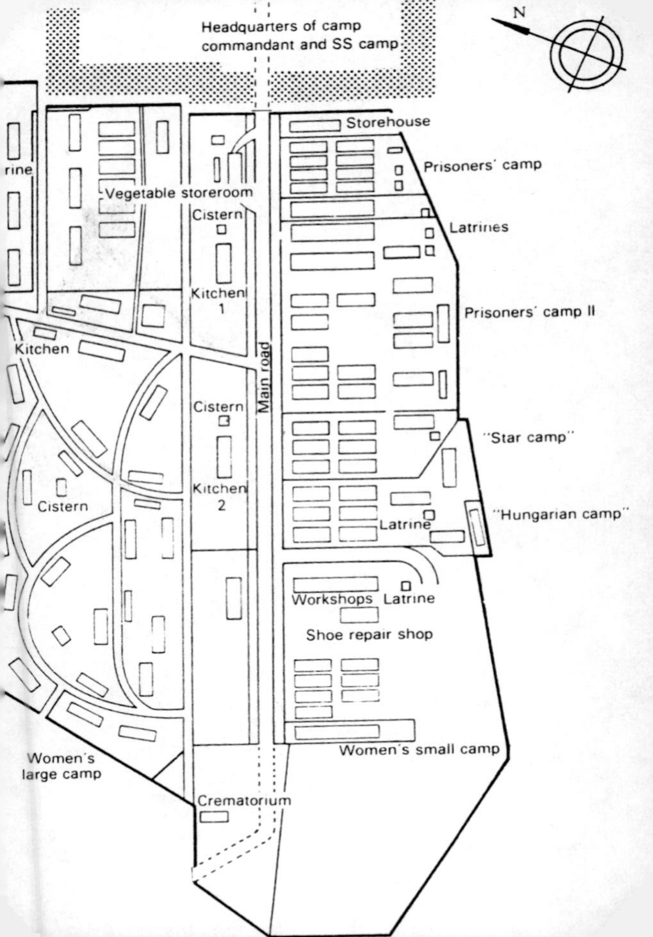
N
Headquarters of camp
commandant and SS camp
Storehouse
Prisoners' camp
rine
Vegetable storeroom
Cistern
Latrines
Kitchen
1
Prisoners' camp II
Kitchen
Main road
Cistern
"Star camp"
Kitchen
2
Cistern
"Hungarian camp"
Latrine
Workshops
Latrine
Shoe repair shop
Women's small camp
Women's
large camp
Crematorium

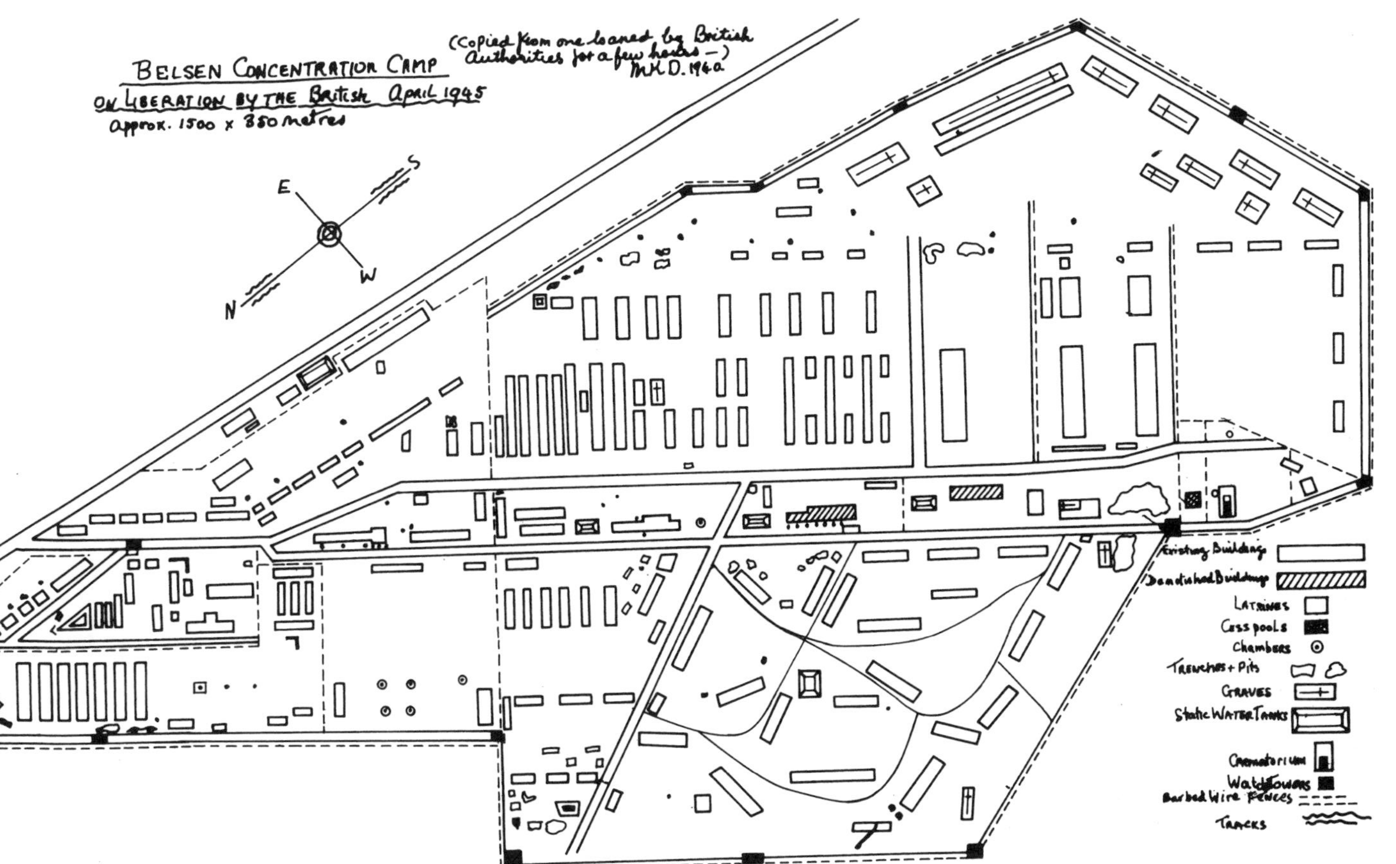

Sketch map of the Belsen Concentration Camp, 1945

UNRRA Operational Unit
Belsen
July 1945

My letters are terribly patchy for they are written at odd intervals in the early morn or well into the night and often by candlelight. I have been told that neither words nor photographs could ever describe the scene which the British found when they entered Camp 1. I have talked with some of the Army, British Red Cross, St John's Ambulance and other personnel who were here in the early days of liberation. They have told me that although it was known that a terrible calamity had occurred and that a typhus epidemic was raging, not one of them imagined that it would be possible to find a scene so horrible in these civilised times. Filth, stench, decomposition and frightfulness abounded—the very air was polluted. The terrible smell was wafted to the approaching troops four miles away down the road, and to the RAF flying overhead. It permeated everything. Forty thousand starving humans, in the most awful state of emaciation and neglect and suffering from practically every known disease, were huddled together, dying in thousands daily. Many were naked, all were verminous. Ten thousand naked unburied dead, some of whom had been decomposing for three weeks, lay in gruesome piles throughout the camp. Thousands were too ill to move and lay where they fell. Numbness and despair enveloped all.

There were five main compounds in this camp—three for men and two for women—divided by barbed wire and containing 28 000 women and 12 000 men. In the larger enclosure for women there were 500 children and only 50 yards away piles of naked dead. The huts were so crowded that the inmates were often unable to lie down and were obliged to sit up round the walls. Countless numbers were without even this shelter. Masses of dead remained where they fell or were pushed under the floorboards to make room for the living—who were beyond caring. Each of the two- and three-tiered wooden bunks held five or six living sick mingled with corpses, which owing to weakness and despair, the living were unable to remove; other sick lay naked on the polluted floor or were wrapped in rags foul with excreta and lice. The Nazis had done practically nothing for the sick for months, and several of the huts which were so-called hospitals were even without bunks. Conditions were worse in the men's than the women's hospitals, although they had more bunks.

Typhus cases were not separated from others. Women opened abscesses with their sharpened fingernails. There were no organised treatment rooms in the camp, just neglect, callousness and cruelty. Latrines were practically non-existent. There were only a few unscreened pits with a pole across. There were no facilities in the huts for washing. Diarrhoea was rampant. Those lying in the lower bunks had no protection from the excreta dripping from above. On the floors the excrement was six inches deep, mixed with rubbish and rags. The walls were heavily contaminated also. You may shudder at these descriptions—perhaps you will say it is sordid and unnecessary. Read on, my friends! The world should know what suffering and degradation this New Order in Europe brought to millions, lest it be quickly forgotten and rise again in yet another guise. It concerns us all—we must not forget—whether you can forgive, you only must decide.

These wretched people had received no supplies of food or drinking water for about six or seven days prior to liberation, after a long period of deliberate and slow starvation. Their ration depended on the whim of the guards. When issued, it consisted of about half a litre of watery swede soup per day and a small portion of a loaf of dark, sour, very hard bread. No food at all was issued during the last week. Is it any wonder that there was evidence of human flesh being eaten by humans?

The lack of water at the time of liberation resulted from an act of sabotage carried out by the Germans during the truce which they requested before handing over the camp. Four German planes bombed and machine-gunned the British Ambulances, the water supply and electricity system of the camp. A pump in the camp was found surrounded by 300–400 bodies, piled up where the thirsty had fallen in a vain attempt to obtain water.

Their end was hastened by the rifle butts and lashings of the SS guards and the sniping of the Hungarian troops. The only drinking water these wretched people had at this time was scooped out of filthy pools, foul and thick with decomposing human flesh and excrement. Conditions had deteriorated in the camp during the last three months. At this time the Germans brought to Belsen a train load of Hungarian prisoners whom they knew were suffering from typhus. I believe, since then, six epidemics had spread through the camp. The numbers who died will never be known. In spite of the agreement with the British liberators, all camp records were destroyed by the SS during the truce. Thousands and perhaps hundreds of thousands died there and their relatives will never know their fate. Many of those who were dying when the British came were too ill to even remember their names and so forever remain unnamed and unknown, but not forgotten.

In spite of the fact that it is said the Panzer troops were forbidden to visit the SS guards at Camp No. 1 and vice versa, one finds it difficult to believe that the horrors which existed in that camp were unknown to those living in the neighbourhood.

I was puzzled, when I saw the patients for the first time, that there was not more evidence of vitamin deficiency. It was therefore interesting to read that Dr Meiklejohn, a member of the Rockefeller Foundation Health Commission who was called in to advise on the nutrition problems of the camp, considered that although three-quarters of the inmates were in a state of marked emaciation (as photographs show) and suffering from protein deficiency, the vitamin deficiency diseases were extremely rare. (I do not know what scientific reason has been given for this.) Among the survivors there was apparently little or no evidence of Vitamin A deficiency or scurvy, but Vitamin B deficiency was seen.

Chapter 4

RESTORATION: EMERGENCY MEASURES

F. Tannenbaum, 'Life in Concentration Camp' series, Belsen, 1945

Belsen
July 1945

Things are beginning to move in a somewhat sluggish fashion but there is still no sign of my staff, so I shall finish my story of Belsen's early days before telling you of my present work and worries. I know you will be anxious to hear how the relatively small group of liberators dealt with the situation they found in the camp, so I shall commence another screed.

A policy was adopted that the greatest number of lives would be saved by placing those who had a reasonable chance of survival under conditions in which the natural tendency to recover would be aided by suitable feeding and prevention of further infection, with rest in bed and elementary nursing for the very sick, and so it was decided to evacuate Camp 1.

The work ahead must have appeared almost insurmountable. No praise is too high for those men and women who by their courage, energy, initiative and perseverance brought to the survivors of this horror, tragedy and suffering—food and drink, cleanliness, sympathy and some glimmer of hope for the future.

One of the doctors who had been a prisoner in the Horror Camp for about four months has said that in January 1945 there was very little food, but the quality was not so bad—what each individual got depended upon his ability to collect. Each person got one-sixth of a loaf of black bread daily—a whole loaf weighed 1.4kg—and sometimes potatoes and pieces of meat, the whole amounting to less than 800 calories. On Sunday, tinned meat was issued—one tin for twelve persons, but this rarely reached the prisoners as there was much pilfering by the Nazi and Hungarian personnel. In February 1945 the food deteriorated, everyone became very thin and typhus broke out. In March the prisoners received one-twelfth of a loaf each, less than three ounces, and in April no bread at all.

Two weeks before liberation the only food the prisoners received was less than one pint of mangel-wurzel soup daily. We also know that no food or water was provided for at least four or five days before liberation and that the water supply was sabotaged by the Germans several times during the truce. As a result of long-standing starvation, the prisoners' bodies were adapted to a low intake of food and water, nevertheless the majority were actually starving on liberation.

The immediate task therefore was to provide water and food for the 40 000. This emergency feeding was a colossal undertaking for the Liberation Army authorities, as you can imagine. Here was a tiny neutral area with vital battles raging all round. Here were some 28 000 living sick, lying amongst heaps of decomposing corpses, and some 16 000 starving men in the nearby Panzer Barracks. Thousands were so ill that they were quite unable to move or feed themselves, and as there was no one to do this for them, they just died.

At first, owing to lack of personnel it was only possible to deliver food from the cook-houses to the doors of the huts. You will understand that by the time the British came the morale of the prisoners was completely broken by their terrible experiences of the preceding weeks. For some time the struggle for existence had been a matter of survival of the fittest and every man for himself. Those who were able to crawl to the doors ate all the food—those too ill to move just went without. The result of this was that very many of the former became dangerously ill with acute diarrhoea and severe vomiting, which caused dehydration and death from overfeeding. Those within the huts died from starvation because there was no one to feed them. I believe the cries of 'Essen, Essen' ('Food, Food') were heart-rending.

I am not in a position, owing to the many changes in medical and nursing staff since the day of liberation, to discuss in detail the scientific feeding of the starving or the nutritional disorders associated with this condition. However the facts I have ascertained from various sources will, I am sure, be of interest to you.

During the truce a British Army-revised daily ration scale for the sick was drawn up by officials of the 32nd CCS and became effective on 14th April, the day before the camp was taken over. My nursing colleagues will be interested in a few details. This scale was divided into three. Scale No. 1 was for starvation and serious febrile cases in two-hourly feeds. Scale No. 2 was for fully convalescent patients and hospital workers. Scale No. 3 was for hospital patients not fully convalescent. The items on Scale 1 were one ounce of sugar, half an ounce of salt, two litres of skimmed fresh milk, and three compound vitamin tablets. Fresh milk was not available in sufficient quantities for all, so skimmed dried milk was used. Forty tons of this were brought in as soon as possible. As you can imagine, fats are not easily tolerated by starving people so that is why the skimmed milk was used.

The reconstitution of dried milk under army conditions was not satisfactory and upset the internees. They thought it caused their diarrhoea and vomiting (which was probably due to starvation) and refused to take it, complaining bitterly. This also was one reason why the rich soup first made had to be modified. Later, biscuits and jam were available in larger quantities and satisfied many of the inmates. It was found that the repetition of the same food for long became nauseating, and providing a variety presented yet another problem. Many of the ex-prisoners had such sore mouths that they found it very difficult and painful to eat.

One week after liberation, Colonel V. P. Sydenstricker, head of the nutrition section of the UNRRA Health Division, Dr C. N. Leach of the Rockefeller Foundation, and Senior RAMC Officers from 21st Army Group visited Belsen Camp. As a result of this conference, Dr A. P. Meiklejohn was seconded to the nutrition section of UNRRA, and arrived at Belsen on 29th April.

When the patients were unable to take the skimmed milk, a mixture which had been used in the Bengal famine (in 1943) was used. Dried milk, flour, sugar, salt and water were cooked in the Army boilers. Glucose drinks to which vitamins were added were also given with the Bengal mixture, one litre of which was sufficient nutrition for one man for a day.

The internees first welcomed this but after a day or two complained that it was too sweet. They had a craving for sour things and would have drunk quantities of vinegar had it been available! They were very difficult to please. Protein hydrolysate treatment was used, but I understand it was also found disappointing. It was out of the question to use it in the filthy huts in Camp 1 (the Horror Camp) and there were not the staff to deal with it in the new hospitals in Camps 2 and 3.

Protein hydrolysate may be given by mouth, by intra-nasal drip, or intravenously. I understand it has an unpleasant taste and smell, so that even when flavoured it was found to be nauseating by mouth, irritating and uncomfortable by nose and not very well tolerated intravenously. When a mixture, it is absorbed at once without the aid of digestive juices, which are often lacking in starvation.

I am told that it has been established that experiments were carried out by German doctors on some prisoners by giving them intravenous injections of benzol and creosote. This explains their terror when the British wished to give them the intravenous hydrolysate. When the staff wished to move them to a special hut for treatment, they cried out, '*Nix crematorium, Nix crematorium*,' and begged not to taken. You see, many awaiting their turn for the gas chamber in Auschwitz had been forced to watch their relatives taken away to the extermination camps and were therefore suspicious of the British stretcher bearers. You can understand how all these problems complicated the treatment and work. This also accounts for the large quantity of casein hydrolysate found unused in the dispensary store-room when I arrived.

In spite of all these problems and disappointments the patients were genuinely grateful and the British persevered. Although the prisoners were dying at the rate of 1000 a day at first, those who lived gradually were able to take solid foods of the type usually given to patients suffering from peptic ulcer. Those on a full diet craved for white bread, which was very scarce, but the British endeavoured to provide as much as possible. However, I have been told that the Russian soldiers, who were also at Belsen at that time, commandeered the white bread for themselves at gunpoint. And got it!

Of course every day the feeding was becoming more organised and more volunteers were arriving. Ninety-six London medical students who had volunteered for relief work in Europe were being held in readiness to move into Holland at this time. It was considered however, that they were most urgently needed at Belsen, and on 30th April, the first began to arrive by air.

On 2nd May the students began distributing food to the 10 000 who were still starving in Camp 1. I believe the psychological effect of the students working there was enormous. They said that after a week they found women crying because another woman had died, and they felt they had achieved something. Each student was responsible for one or more huts with 100–150 helpless patients and about 200–300 so-called fit—those who were able to feed themselves.

One student, with two Hungarian guards (British POWs now) to assist him, worked in co-operation with the officers in charge of the six cook-houses and travelled round with the food vans, delivering the food to their colleagues in the huts—this enabled a fair distribution of food to be made. Gradually the more fit internees were able to assist with the feeding and nursing of the sick. It was, of course, impossible to keep the patients in bed, as without any warning they would leave suddenly to taste their new-found freedom. I heard that one old woman clad in nothing but a blanket flowing from her shoulders was found at the gates, setting out for Poland!

One student has written that an old man with a gastric ulcer was put on a milk diet and alkalis and lost his pain. Relieved from pain and feeling rather hungry, he staggered outside to the dustbin, ate what he could find there, plus any berries on the bushes on the way, and returned to *Herr Doktor* groaning again!

Fresh bread was a joy not experienced for a long time

Belsen
July 1945

Although we have not yet taken over the hospitals, my days are very full as there is so much organising to be done in preparation for the arrival of our staff. My letters seem to be very scrappy, but I find the best time for writing is after the curfew has tolled—and so I shall now continue my story of how the gallant liberators worked. While one little group of warm-hearted, patient, generous and sympathetic British Tommies was dealing with the enormous feeding problem, other workers were preparing for the evacuation of the Horror Camp.

The Wehrmacht troops were turned out of the German barracks, but I have not been able to find out whether they were taken prisoner or whether they fled. The German sick were transferred first to the German Officer's Club and later to another German hospital in the district, and we are told the occupants of the married quarters had disappeared! Our troops distributed ground sheets, on which groups of people who were unable to find room inside the huts in Camp 1 lived until they could be evacuated.

Parties of armed British troops then collected, at gunpoint where necessary, from German residents and stores in the surrounding district all the equipment they could find for a 17 000-bed emergency hospital in the barracks. Just imagine the quantities of beds, bedding, drugs, surgical dressings, food and hospital equipment which had to be found!

Colonel Johnstone's anaesthetist of the 32nd British Casualty Clearing Station was in charge of the collection and distribution of supplies. A nursing and domestic staff on a huge scale also had to be organised from the inmates of the camp who were well enough, and from the German population, Barracks personnel, and Hungarian troops. On 20th April, the day this hospital was ready for use, the Germans again sabotaged the water supply before they left, and delayed the transfer of patients for twenty-four hours.

Before leaving Camp 1, all inmates who were considered fit were taken to a large building, all their clothing removed and burnt and their bodies cleansed of the gross filth and deloused. A colossal undertaking, dusting some 30–40 000 people with DDT powder! Women and children were evacuated first and a shuttle ambulance service was constantly moving. Quite soon, but I cannot find out the date, one of the medical officers had an inspiration and set up a cleansing station called the human laundry in one of the barracks stables in Camp 3. Six tables were arranged in two rows to receive those direct from the Horror Camp. British Tommies supervised German nurses and attendants, who were obliged to cleanse, wash and dust these poor naked and ill creatures, cut their hair and wrap them in three fresh blankets.

Many were horrified and cried with fear when they heard they were to be taken to the bath, because, as I have told you, in Auschwitz and other extermination camps many had been marched to the showers from which came lethal gas. Numbers, of course, were too ill and dazed to care what happened to them at this stage.

The ambulances conveyed the sick direct from the huts in Camp 1 to the laundry, as well as the walking cases who had received some preliminary cleansing in that camp. Five hundred to 900 were treated daily. These unfortunate creatures, mere skeletons with but a spark of life in them, were then conveyed in a decontaminated ambulance to the squares where the first emergency hospitals were established.

The sick were then placed naked (there were at this stage no bed garments) in their blankets on a straw palliasse, on a barracks stretcher or on one of the bunks. The Sisters and their voluntary assistants fed them and gave such nursing care as was possible under the circumstances.

By 30th April the whole population of the camp had been deloused and by 1st May 7000 sick had been evacuated to the new hospital area. There were, however, still approximately 10 000 patients in Camp 1 requiring urgent medical attention, for whom no hospital accommodation could be provided for some days.

The male members of the British Red Cross Society, RAMC doctors, the London medical students, British troops, and doctors and nurses from among the displaced persons in the camp who were fit to work carried on in the intense squalor of the Horror Camp. They fed and nursed the patients, cleansing huts, rendering first aid and performing minor operations. I believe Miss Beardwell, a Sister from St George's Hospital, London, was in charge of the first 600 patients to be admitted to the new hospital. She is now in charge of the BRCS staff at the Children's Hospital here. When the medical students commenced work, they moved the corpses, set up a dispensary and gave medical treatment to the sick in the huts. Assisted by groups of internees and the Hungarian guards, they endeavoured to clean out the worst of the filth which lay inches deep on the floors. You can imagine just how difficult their work was, because the weather was very hot and flies were beginning to appear.

Twenty-five of these students—led by Captain Crips, MC King's Royal Rifles, one of the senior students—under the direction of the RAMC officer in charge, created within the Horror Camp a hospital area in which the most seriously ill were nursed until they could be evacuated. They cleansed the filthy, verminous huts, creosoting the floors, disinfecting with DDT and equipping them with the necessities of a hospital ward. They set up a marquee which was used as a cleansing station for all patients before they were admitted to the new hospital. There was difficulty in washing these people because the women refused to wash the men and all the men were too weak to do this. So the students, assisted by the Hungarian guards, undertook this as well as the multitude of other urgent matters requiring attention. One week after the arrival of the students, the death rate was halved, and in two weeks halved again. Within two weeks of the setting up of the hospital in Camp 1, 12 000 patients had been washed, disinfected, admitted, treated and nursed. It has been authoritatively stated that a large number of patients owe their lives to this achievement. This venture was so successful that the hospital was allowed to function until all the other patients in Camp 1 had been transferred to the Barracks.

The students eventually evacuated the patients, equipment and nurses to the very palatial Round House, where it is said such high-ranking Nazi officials as Himmler, Goering and Goebbels had once been entertained. On 19th May the last survivors of the 28 000 persons were evacuated from the notorious Horror Camp to the hospitals and three transit camps in the Barracks area. Up to that time the British had supervised the burial of some 23 000 of which, you will remember, 10 000 or even more, lay unburied when they arrived on 15th April.

SS Guards, men and women, watched by groups of internees,

were forced to carry out the work of burying the dead. Bulldozers were used to dig the enormous graves, each of which contained from 500 to 5000 bodies. The SS women were unmoved by the awfulness of this task and I have a photo showing one, actually smiling, as she unloaded the scores and scores of naked corpses into the pits. The men cringed and shrank from the task.

The daily death rate steadily decreased. On 30th April, 548 people had died; on 17th May ninety-seven; but by 18th May, 13 834 patients had been admitted to hospital.

On 19th May there took place the historic ceremonial burning of the last hut in the infamous Belsen Concentration Camp, one of the most terrible concentration camps set up by the Nazis.

On 21st May 1945, at 6 pm, the day on which quarantine was lifted, Colonel H. L. Bird, Commanding 102 Control Section 2nd Army, addressed those assembled from a dais equipped with a microphone—with him were Colonel J. A. D. Johnstone and Brigadier Glyn Hughes. An invitation was given to personnel and to all displaced persons who wished to attend. Transport was arranged and a large number came, including all the British troops and dozens of cinema and press reporters. I was told that the ceremony was simple and satisfying. Fauna Campbell and a Queensland nurse, Miss Jean MacDougall-Ind, and a Major Prior, another Australian, were present at this ceremony. Unfortunately, the Sergeant driving one of the flame-throwers accidentally pressed the button and the fire started before the speeches were made, so that the ceremony was delayed while the fire was extinguished.

Colonel Bird explained that the British flag never stood for cruelty and bestiality—that was why it had never yet flown over Belsen Camp. He continued:

> I cannot help feeling that in the razing of this pestilence-ridden camp, there is a great symbol. It is a symbol of the final destruction for all time, of the bestial human creed of Nazi Germany; a creed by which criminals tried to debase the people of Europe to their own devilish ends. This moment is the end of the chapter—the pages of which are filled with the vilest story of cruelty, hate and bestiality ever written by man. British soldiers have closed one chapter and by their great efforts have opened a new chapter in the lives of the survivors. I would like to pay special tribute to the British soldier—his great heart, his

> patience, his sympathy and his sense of humour have always made him the finest Ambassador any nation could wish for.

A party of soldiers then fired a salute to the dead and Brigadier Glyn Hughes and Colonel Johnstone each directed a flame-thrower onto a portrait of Adolf Hitler at one end of the hut and a huge Nazi flag at the other. A thick black column of smoke showed everyone that Camp 1 was no more, and amid cheers and cat calls which completely drowned the official cheering, the last hut was reduced to ashes. The Union Jack, symbol of British justice, freedom and protection of the oppressed, was then unfurled, caught in the breeze and fluttered over the scene.

Thus concluded the first phase in the history of Belsen since its liberation by the British. The work carried out by doctors, nurses, medical students, Army personnel, British Red Cross, St John's Ambulance teams and International relief missions in those early days is said to be one of the most remarkable achievements in medical history.

Belsen
20th July 1945

We have been here nine days now and are champing at the bit. Most of my time is spent in the hospitals, but I am taking the opportunity to make all the contacts I can before actually taking over. Today I was driven to the site of the former No. 1 Camp by Mr Simmonds, a member of St John's Ambulance who was one of the original workers here. I have already mentioned that the camp is surrounded by lovely forests of spruce, birch and beeches. As we approached I saw evidence of the habitation in the woods, of those whose home it had so recently been. The camp itself was entirely surrounded by two sets of heavy barbed wire. Immediately outside this prison wall were fourteen watch-towers, situated at intervals all the way round; nearby but also outside the camp were deep shelters for the guards. There was no provision for the protection of the internees during air raids.

Having satisfied the British guard that we had authority to enter and that we had been inoculated against typhus, we drove to the first area, carefully wired off by the Germans for their administrative and personnel section, which was housed in the usual army type of hutted buildings and provided with fifteen shower baths for the guards and administrative personnel. On the right was a large stable or garage in which all those entering and leaving camp after liberation were dusted with DDT. At the entrance to the actual concentration area where the British found the 50 000 living and dead huddled together in filth, disease, decomposition and despair, are two large notice boards. One in English on the left, the other on the right in German. They state: 'This is the site of the Infamous Belsen Concentration Camp liberated by the British on 15th April 1945. Ten thousand unburied dead were found here, another 13 000 have since died, all of them victims of the German New Order in Europe and an example of Nazi *Kultur.*'

We passed on and walked through the former dispensary, dressing rooms, and the room where the minor operations were performed. All was chaotic; quantities of damaged medical equipment, furniture, rags and paper littered the floors, evidence of the enormous amount of work carried out after liberation. We passed the building where the fit were cleansed and deloused before being transferred to the transit camp. A nauseating odour still pervaded these buildings.

We saw the charred remains of the burnt-out huts with only a few odd bits of china and metal to mark the site. The enormous mass graves holding uncertain numbers, but from 500 to 5000 bodies again reminded us of Nazi brutality and inhumanity.

In a hollow at the far end of the camp the tall chimney of the crematorium with its metal cradle and long-handled stoker, among the powdered remains of the unknown, needed no explanation. Nearby an enormous pile of half burnt leather boots and shoes of all sizes is a silent reminder of the thousands who entered the camp, but did not leave. There are several mass graves in pits earthed over in this vicinity.

The pump where so many were beaten to death as they crawled in search of water was evident. A relic of the blue-and-white striped prison garb, with a large yellow cross branded on the back, was stretched on the barbed wire fence. Outside the camp we had seen the remains of a drum of yellow paint.

The medical students' hospital is now a charred mass. Huge camp ovens, cauldrons and sets of new wooden toilet fixtures brought in by the British are still there.

An erection which could have been a gibbet was in full view of the camp. Two poles mark the site where the final burning ceremony took place and from which the portrait of Hitler and the flag with the crooked cross had been suspended. The platform from which the speeches were made still stands.

The SS Guards' quarters were wired off and well protected from the inmates of the camp. The stone prison is in this area, heavily protected by barbed wire even on the small windows where it was interlaced with the iron bars. A large dog kennel marked the HQ of the savage dogs which patrolled the area between the building and barriers, and which were let loose on the prisoners according to the whim of the men and women SS guards.

From this point I surveyed the devastated camp—a foul blot in a picturesque countryside. The air was charged with a ghostly silence. I closed my eyes and saw it all and no longer found it hard to believe that it had actually happened. So many victims were still in our own hospital wards. I felt nothing we could do for them could ever compensate. Never was there greater scope for UNRRA's relief and rehabilitation.

To: Miss Udell, Chief Nursing Adviser, UNRRA
Date: 16th July 1945

I intend to arrange for my staff to have an eight-hour day, with one day off duty per week, providing no further emergency occurs. So to do this under existing circumstances I shall require, in addition to myself:

One assistant to the Matron, preferably English-speaking.
Fifteen general trained nurses including:

(a) one or more qualified as midwife, one of whom would be capable of eventually taking over the Maternity Hospital
(b) one with experience in Children's Nursing capable of taking charge of the Children's Hospital later
(c) one or more with experience in Tb nursing
(d) one or more who has had experience in Operating Theatre techniques, to supervise the German Theatre staff

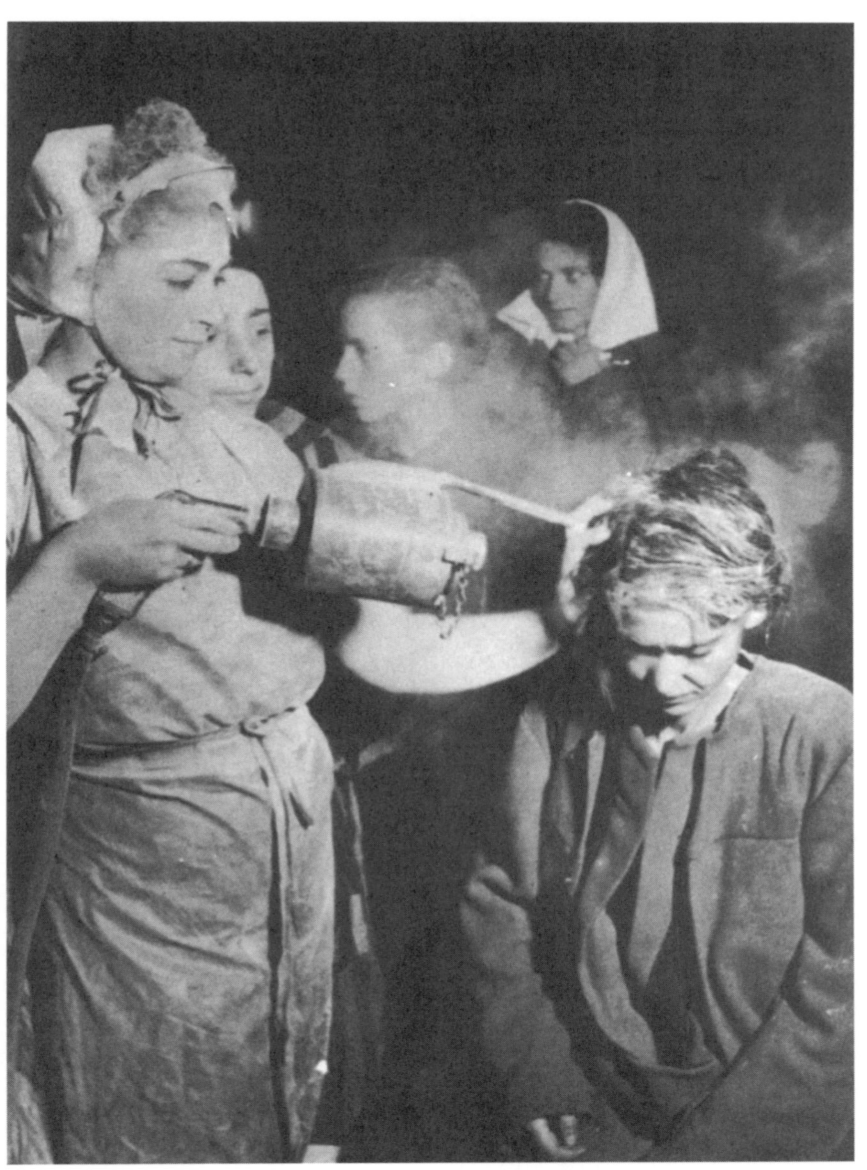

A nurse disinfecting a survivor with DDT in an attempt to combat typhus

Belsen
29th July 1945

Eighteen days since our arrival, and many an SOS has gone forth, both to London and local HQ, but nary a body have I seen in the way of UNRRA nursing staff!

You will have received my letters outlining the early history of Belsen. My future screeds will, I hope, give you some idea of the conditions prevailing upon and after my arrival. The early days of phase two were those of intense and exhausting work for the staff and of miraculous change for the patients. Doctors, nurses, and all other personnel were toiling from morn till night in the Squares, the Round House, the Glyn Hughes and children's Hospitals. Mr Winston Churchill's famous tribute to the RAF in the Battle for Britain might well apply to these courageous people.

I have talked with a number of the original liberators and have been impressed by the modest way in which they narrate their experiences. Feeding the victims of starvation and disease was in itself a colossal and oft times heartbreaking undertaking. The moment food appeared, those who could, oblivious of their stark nakedness, staggered forward from their beds, gaunt spectres, with arms outstretched, crying, '*Essen, essen.*' ('Food, food'.) They sometimes criticised the small quantities of food served, some said they were better off under the Germans when they had their watery soup and morsel of dry bread. They were not sufficiently mentally fit, as yet, to appreciate the fact that their diet was highly nutritious. Others were at first fearful of being looked after by the German nurses, even under Allied supervision, and cried out at the sight of the simplest apparatus. They now mostly take the Germans for granted, although we do have some difficulties at times, when we have to investigate accusations of neglect and stealing food.

Just imagine Bofors' gunner officers suddenly finding themselves appointed as chief chefs and having to cope with this colossal job, assisted by willing displaced persons, workers of all nationalities all speaking different languages. The full diet consisted of thick meat and vegetable soup with boiled potatoes, thrice daily, black bread and a very small quantity of jam and cheese—but even this was too rich and frequently caused vomiting. Very few ate the black bread, but the potatoes were popular. The fit people spent most of the day re-cooking little bits of food on little fires all over the camp—we even see this done today in the hospital by those who have acquired small electric cookers! It is common for a savoury odour to be wafted down the corridor and to find, on investigation, a little group of eager women clustered round a precious mug full of some mysterious egg concoction, or mushroom delicacy. They just love it.

To return to my story of the camp—the workers were given meals at an improvised canteen in the camp. Another problem of feeding was to see that the soup reached the more fit people and that the bland mixture was given to the sick—which, at first, was almost impossible. Having relieved starvation, the next work for the British was to restore to convalescence those who were fortunate enough to recover and to bring such comfort as was possible to those destined to lead a life of invalidism and those whose days were numbered. Fauna Campbell, in a letter, describes the wards in those early days:

> Each of us is in charge of blocks of 150 patients, speaking foreign languages. In the first block I took over, I had a Polish doctor, Polish and Russian nurses recovering from illness, and patients from Poland, Russia, France, Italy, Czechoslovakia, etc. Many were Jews, nearly all so weak and such absolute skeletons, with a sad hunted expression, ravenous for food. Never shall I forget those poor little faces peeping out from their blankets, and their tiny bodies lying on palliasses of straw, with the habits more or less of animals. The stench, I feel, will never leave my nostrils.
>
> My staff is entirely German, with the exception of one British orderly and four Hungarian soldiers for cleaning. Typhus, typhoid, mouth, gastro-intestinal and skin infections, scabies, pulmonary tuberculosis, bronco-pneumonia, famine oedema, large pressure sores, suppurating wounds and gangrene were some of the complaints from which the patients were suffering. Diarrhoea was almost universal. In the early days all were crying, '*Schwester* (Sister), *Fräulein* (Miss), Madame, basin, *pfanne* (pan), *schüssel* (bowl).'

They begged continuously for an operation, for medicines or for their dressing to be done. There were insufficient nurses at first to feed all the helpless or to encourage those with poor appetites, so that often food was left untouched. The stronger, still haunted by the fear of starvation, hoarded what they could among their bedding. Some still continue to do this. It was some time before they regained confidence and appreciated the fact that when they had eaten the food provided, another meal would appear in a few hours.

The German nurses, I am told, appeared shocked at what they saw when first brought to the hospital and they worked quite well under close supervision. The death rate was still high. A board outside each block indicated the number of deaths during the day. The bodies were placed in the cellars and collected in wagons at 6 pm; new cemeteries began to appear. Although thousands died, thousands more had been brought back to health by the devoted and untiring attention of those privileged to care for them.

The thing which we sincerely hope is that those who have no home, no families and no country to which to return, and who have had everything that was worthwhile in their lives taken from them and have been through hell, will find sympathy and understanding in whatever country they finally settle. It is only in this way they can hope to recover from their sick minds and broken bodies and start life afresh. I do not think they will ever forget the tortures, the atrocities and the mental agonies through which they have passed, but it will be made easier for them if they feel they are wanted and welcome in their new homes. It was wonderful for those working amongst the patients to see their returning interest in their appearance and their joy at receiving their first hair comb, soap, tooth brush, or bit of chocolate. Sewing materials gave great joy as they became stronger and clever fingers fashioned many a garment. Those who were convalescent would gather huge armfuls of lupins from the nearby fields or bunches of greenery, and with tit-bits of food would hand them through the windows to their less fortunate friends in hospital.

Nursing conditions were primitive and the wards over-crowded. There were insufficient bed-pans, practically no sputum mugs, and drugs were in hopelessly short supply in the early days. If one patient got a pill, all had to receive a pill and the only ones available were aspirin and opium tablets. There were insufficient sheets for changing the beds—improvisation was carried out to the last degree.

Thousands of patients were in the advanced stages of tuberculosis and it was impossible at first to separate them from the typhus cases; others were still dehydrated and exhausted. The lack of interpreters made nursing extremely difficult.

The typhus blocks in Camp 3 were surrounded with barbed wire and the main squares took the general cases. There was also a Mental House. Three blocks were converted into maternity and children's hospitals where women suffering from typhus were confined. The doctor in charge of the Maternity Hospital was a Romanian Jewess, who told me that at Auschwitz she had been forced to deliver and then kill all babies born. You could see she was suffering from this experience. She told me that she had been present at 1000 births.

The British wing, as it was called, in the Glyn Hughes Hospital, at first housed a number of orderlies and RAMC men who contracted typhus. I think there were ten altogether, but all recovered. About fifty ex-enemy personnel also contracted the disease and a number died.

The organisation of the new camp was amazing—accommodation had to be arranged for the patients as they were discharged from the hospital, for those who had not been admitted to hospital, and for the slave workers from the surrounding districts, whom the British by this time were bringing into the camp. Camp 3 housed the patients able to work and partly look after themselves and the convalescents. All were very weak and were frequently re-admitted to hospital.

Nationalities and relatives were housed as far as possible together. This interesting, yet tragic community was a hive of activity. These displaced persons had to be fed and clothed and housed. As each one was discharged from hospital he or she was taken, swathed in blankets to Harrods, the clothing store in the charge of the BRCS, and fitted out with clothing.

Registration had to be carried out, food ration cards to be issued, and information offices to be set up to assist in tracing relatives and friends. You will remember I told you that all camp records were destroyed by the SS guards during the truce, although the agreement was that everything was to be handed over intact.

Army ration and ordinance stores, laundry, cookhouses, food and clothing distribution centres, dispensaries, and first aid rooms also had to be organised. Sanitary squads were constantly busy—

a steady stream of transport was kept moving. Ambulance services never ceased. Grave-diggers were constantly at work. Planes were repatriating the fit. Welfare officers worked unceasingly and postal services were soon set up. Liaison Officers of many nations began to arrive. Their work was to discuss with displaced persons of their own nationality their repatriation, and to provide information about conditions in their home countries. Personnel from many international voluntary organisations and special relief missions commenced work. A number of Belgian medical students came with the Belgian mission to Belsen.

The DPs came and went as they liked, their registration cards being the only thing necessary to enable them to pass the guards at the gates. Before going any further, a few words about the DPs may interest you. These men, women and children were displaced outside their own national territories, as forced labourers, refugees from battle zones, anti-Nazi exiles, victims of persecution, prisoners of concentration camps.

At Belsen today there are families, old people, young men, women and children, babies, orphans of the concentration camps and unaccompanied children (children whose parents' whereabouts are unknown). There are Jews and Christians and, on liberation, British, Czechs, Romanians, Poles, French, Dutch, Belgians, Russians, Germans, Gypsies, Austrians, Italians, Danes, Yugoslavs, Greeks, Norwegians, Latvians, Lithuanians, Estonians, Hungarians and other nationals. One has only to walk round the cemeteries in this camp to see the nations represented.

As soon as they were fit to travel, thousands were repatriated by the army authorities, in conjunction with their own Governments, to receive further hospitalisation in their own countries. A bomber shuttle service carried out this work. Thousands more have made their own way home voluntarily and unassisted, but thousands who are stateless, homeless, and many without hope still remain. Why do they remain?, you will ask. The answer is that they are unwilling or unable to return to their own countries or their former place of residence. Some are ignorant of the conditions prevailing in their country, and some know too much about them and feel that there is no future there if they do return—no jobs, no homes. Others wish to start a new life in another part of the world and forget their sufferings.

Many hold political views incompatible with the present regime in their own countries. Poles, having been members of the underground resistance movement when Russia was Germany's ally, and others who had escaped from imprisonment in the Soviet or Soviet-occupied Poland say it is unsafe for them to return to their country while it is under Soviet domination.

The Jews, whatever their country of origin (and the majority here at present are from Poland), knowing that they are practically the sole survivors of their race in Europe are anxious to leave the European continent and start life anew. Their eyes are already turning towards Palestine, whither their destiny leads them. Some Poles and others look towards the United Kingdom and United States of America for freedom and vainly believe that the streets there are paved with gold!

Unless the future of these homeless and stateless people is solved, all the work carried out here and elsewhere will have been in vain. If they are going out into a hostile world to again struggle against overwhelming odds, they might have been better off had they not survived the Nazi terrors of Belsen and other concentration camps.

You will understand that many who have suffered so much at the hands of the Germans, and whose very existence has for so many years depended on astuteness and physical strength, have lost much of their moral sense. After four or five years or longer in a German concentration camp there must inevitably be an increasing selfishness and a lowering of moral standards. Some of them now raid the German farms, houses, shops and villages and are frequently joined by large numbers of other DPs, whom the Nazis had used as slave labourers and who, on cessation of hostilities, downed tools and formed marauding bands, or set up more or less organised colonies throughout Germany. Many of the latter have wandered into this camp. Pillaging is rife. In their opinion they are perfectly justified in robbing the Germans, who, after all, brought most of them into this country and so must take the consequences. Many of the goods they take are of no value to them, but their desire to acquire possessions again is very acute and they must have gained a great deal of satisfaction from being in the position to get a little of their own back. There have been a good many shootings in the nearby forest and surrounding neighbourhood, but a strict order regarding the possession of firearms has recently been issued.

This just about brings me to the time when I arrived at Belsen on 11th July 1945, and closes Phase 2.

I cannot write more tonight. My tasks are many and the work of instituting Phase 3 and transforming an acute emergency hospital into an organised hygienic institution will be arduous but, as you can imagine, I will be in my element.

Chapter 5

SIGNS OF NORMALITY

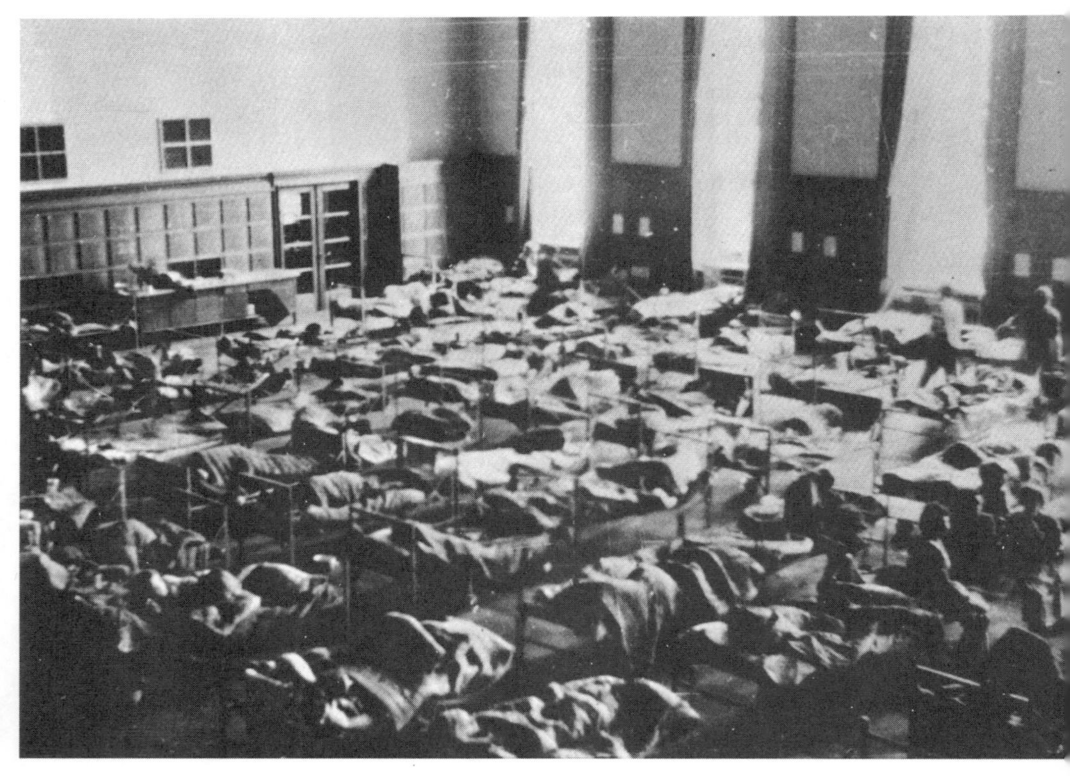

The Round House, the former headquarters of the German Army base in Bergen-Belsen, in which an improvised hospital was set up with hundreds of beds

Belsen Camp Hospital
August 1945

Life is one whirl and writing letters is becoming increasingly difficult. My first work at Belsen, apart from rounds in the hospitals and estimating my requirements for nursing staff, was to make contact with those responsible for the welfare of the DPs and the administration of the camp. The 81st British General Hospital Staff was in control of all the Hospitals, assisted by a unit of BRCS nurses, twenty French Nuns of the Vatican Mission (Franciscan and St Vincent de Paul Orders), twenty Latvians, some DPs and about 150 German nurses, the latter virtual POWs of course.

As I told you, I understood we would be taking over from the Army authorities almost immediately after our arrival, but owing to a frightful muddle over accommodation, protracted delay in arrival of UNRRA staff, and a number of other things quite beyond our control, the date has been postponed on more than one occasion, much to our disgust. It is exasperating, for although there is never one spare minute in the day, as I am co-operating with the British Matron and find plenty to keep me occupied, as you will see, we feel that had the UNRRA medical administration in this Zone pulled itself together a bit more, we could have been in charge much sooner.

So that you will have some idea of what our work entails, I shall give you a brief account of the situation as I found it. There were some thousands of patients in the Squares and the Round House. The advanced cases of pulmonary Tb, many with post-typhus complications, were just packed in every available corner of the latter, including the corridors and cloakrooms—there must have been about 200–300 in the ballroom alone. Beds were side by side and head to foot in endless rows. There were few facilities for nursing these cases—no sterilisers, no sputum mugs, only a few pots, basins and tins, mostly without lids. Disinfectants and soap were very scarce.

I shall never forget the first day I walked round this ward with the QAIMNS Sister and saw the gaunt, emaciated, pallid skeletons, some too ill to observe, others giving a passing smile or glimmer of recognition—a few were brighter. Death was stalking, but no one noticed—death meant nothing to these who had lived, eaten and slept among the dead for so long. There was, of course, no privacy but that, too, was a forgotten thing for most. One saw a nurse or a nun bending over a bed offering perhaps a last word of consolation, then all was still. A Professor from Prague University, or a doctor from Warsaw had passed on.

The modern, 250-bed Glyn Hughes Hospital also held over 2000 patients, with beds in every corridor and alcove and packed into the wards. An army of flies had taken possession; they were everywhere in millions, thriving on the food hoarded by the patients. They occupied the wards and swarmed over everything. There were no mosquito nets and the weak were unable to protect their faces. I knew that would be our first campaign.

Pretty shrubs round the buildings were simply teeming; I itched to collect the DDT squad and get going immediately. Why there had not been an epidemic of gastro-intestinal infections, I know not. The resistance of these people must be high, but there was a considerable number of people suffering from Belsen Tummy who never reached the hospital stage and who probably had the flies to blame. We, ourselves, have been sufferers from time to time.

The children's hospital, in the charge of Professor W. R. F. Collis of Dublin University (and a specialist in paediatrics), with its large marquees to house the overflow, held several hundred little patients, the majority suffering from post-typhus, advanced pulmonary Tb and the results of starvation. I have been told that very few children under two years of age survived in the concentration camp.

Nearly all were orphans. Never have I seen so many children so terribly ill, or so frightfully emaciated. A number, of course, made rapid improvement with proper treatment, but very many died. It made me sick to see even tiny children branded on the lateral aspect of the left forearm with the Auschwitz tattoo identification number, knowing that it had meant the gas chamber eventually.

Franz Berlin was a wee mite picked up in that city after his parents had been killed by a bomb. A Czech driver brought him to Belsen. Some of the children are good artists, and the walls of the wards bear excellent caricatures of Adolf as well as dainty fairy pictures and national flags. A Dutch DP nurse who drew murals

External view of Wards A1 and A3, Glyn Hughes Hospital, Belsen, 1945

rather like those done by our Pixie O'Harris has added her contribution to the grubby plaster.

The gypsy children are sweet and so precocious, with such marked personality—Eva, about four years old but undersized, is particularly fascinating and coquettish, dances beautifully and has learnt quite a lot of English. She takes me by the hand when I arrive at her hospital and leads me to Sister, which she proudly pronounces.

One little boy of five looks after his sister of two—all he has in the world. His parents were murdered by the Germans before his eyes. Another little boy, with paternal concern, jealously guards his two tiny sisters—they do not know where their parents are. Although some children were difficult to discipline at first I am told they quickly lost their terror symptoms and became interested in the life around them. The wooden cots in this Hospital were made by the British Tommies when they liberated the camp. I shall have them copied, if I can, when we furnish our new Maternity wards in the British Wing of the Glyn Hughes Hospital. The original

Maternity Hospital is grossly overcrowded but as far as I can see, this is because the DP doctor in charge has allowed the mothers and babies to become permanent boarders.

While I am marking time I have been trying also to gain an insight into the general life of the DPs here, but this is not always easy as my activities (apart from the time spent in the Hospitals) are punctuated with making arrangements for our mess, staff transport to and from Hospital, staff recreation and DP staff rosters, incoming and outgoing mails, disposal of garbage, free cigarette and matches issue for patients, special gate passes for UNRRA nurses to enter the camp, installation of hospital phones and extermination of mice (with only rat traps available) and flies!

Today I visited Harrods. At first, when the British commandeered clothing and footwear from the surrounding districts of Hanover, things were of good quality and fairly presentable. Later, when the Military Government at Lüneberg ordered a levy of a set of clothes from every German, man, woman and child, and the Burgomaster was responsible for the collection, the quality rapidly deteriorated and the footwear was terrible. The source of supply is drying up now or going underground, and it is very gratifying to know that the people of Australia are making such a splendid effort in their collection of clothes for Europe. You should see some of the underclothes which I saw on Harrods shelves—voluminous combinations of the heavy German type, antiquated chemises and a varied collection of garments no one would wear. However, the DPs are adept with scissors and needles, if only we had sufficient scissors and needles to give them.

I was interested to see a number of DP girls wearing well-cut blue and white gingham dresses when I first arrived, but soon awakened to the fact that, instead of being the donation of some Dorcas Society, they were the converted mattress covers and quilts from the Hospital. We found that as our original patients recovered sufficiently to take an interest in themselves and their surroundings, the creative instinct asserted itself.

The grey costumes and greatcoats so well tailored are our precious blankets, and the hospital sheets make very attractive summer frocks! Curtains, quilts and even a Union Jack have been transformed into wearing apparel, but the enterprising girl who made the smart red, white and blue godet skirt was, I am sorry to say, severely reprimanded by the officials!

These DPs are mostly young, few of the older ones or the intellectuals survived their incarceration. They are clever with their fingers and it is really a good thing that they are taking such a personal interest in their appearance, for it is an indication of their return to normality. Fortunately, in the early stages there were no inventories or linen counts, or the Sister's hair would surely have turned grey.

The system of clothing for all DPs on leaving Hospital now is to give them a chit which they take to Harrods, where they are fitted out. The well DPs who have received one issue and require more are visited in their blocks by a BRCS worker, who, with the DP Block Leader, tours each building and enquires what they want. She well knows that on the day of her coming all surplus clothes have probably been removed to another block, and the oldest and shabbiest are being worn. The bunks, so tidily covered with a blanket or cover, conceal many a garment or collection of food, and it is a study to see the expression on their faces when she turns up a corner or approaches a cupboard.

The first day I went round with her, many women were lying in these two-tiered bunks and still looked ill and wan, a number bore the Auschwitz number tattooed on their forearm. One can understand that these people who have struggled so long for existence still must gather all they can. Wouldn't you? When leaving Harrods the workers run their hands over each one and frequently make a haul of several dresses, stockings or other garments, surreptitiously concealed in armpits, inside coats and under the legitimate bundle of issued clothing carried over their arm. Some even forge the chits issued by the worker after her tour of their apartments, to suit their requirements.

I enjoyed this trip round their homes—some are very neat and tidy, their owners having acquired many articles of furniture from the surrounding district. I told you before that pillaging is rife—the Germans are mostly too terrified to do anything about it. I have seen some good raincoats and costumes which I'm sure did not come out of Harrods. But do you blame them? The Germans brought us here, so must take the consequences, is the general attitude.

This is a crazy place—we sometimes have to protect the Germans from the DPs! A few of the young DPs are extremely lawless and present a major problem. Any control exercised brings the retort that they were better off under the Germans, so that the British efforts to give them freedom are fraught with problems.

The Kindergarten conducted by the BRCS with the help of DP teachers is fascinating. The first day I visited it, the rooms were full of little Titos (as the Yugoslavs are called). The girls were in school and the boys were out walking, as there were insufficient desks for both at a time. Their work is beautiful. They are artistic, neat and painstaking, although the Czech children are considered to be even better. They have a large room, originally the canteen of one of the barracks squares, with gay pictures, and some of their own original pencil and crayon drawings on the walls, with a Punch and Judy show (which I don't consider suitable here), books and sand-pit—in fact a well set up Kindergarten. I feel this education for these children now is terribly important.

There is also a *Kinderheim* [kindergarten] in the camp for the younger children, and a school for the older ones. Woolworths is also very attractive—set up in one of the many large stables, just as Harrods is—for this was at one time a German Cavalry training school. Woolworths houses hardware, linen, blankets and cleaning materials—all of which are exceedingly scarce. The Squares where the DPs live are interesting too and a hive of activity. There are 13 000 living there at present and there will be at least 20 000 for the winter. Nearby, at a DP camp at Falingbostel, there are to be 30 000 Poles shortly!

Everyone of the DPs is, of course, free to arrange the room, in which from four to eight live, as they like and with whatever they can find, in addition to their own issue of blankets and clothing. Some take great interest and have pretty window curtains, table mats, and covers which they keep very clean. I even saw china cabinets, floor rugs, cushions, antimacassars and plush throwovers on beds—others are not so careful. One also sees masses of hard stale rye bread, jugs of queer-looking liquid and basins of curd and other national delicacies!

The food ration at Belsen, which is a reasonably liberal one, is cooked by DPs in the large kitchens attached to the canteens, supervised by a British Army corporal. It is served there but a large number bring basins, jugs and plates and carry it away to concoct into more national or favourite dishes over fires lit near their residences, or on the fuel heating stoves in their rooms. Wooden slats from the bedsteads make good kindling, in fact they burn anything they can find, as long as it's German!

The gypsies here are most artistic and colourful and decorate their rooms with greenery and any coloured bits they come across and are themselves most picturesque and friendly.

The acute emergency stage is passing and I can see that our future job will not only be to do what we can from a medical point of view for those who live, in order to help them to become physically and psychologically able to take part in things again and to regain a normal outlook, but to encourage them to forget the past and grasp the new life which awaits them in the future. This, I am sure, will not be difficult for us in the majority of cases, for already they are exhibiting marked signs of returning interest in themselves and their fellow humans, and a desire to take part in social activities and commence life anew.

There are several large recreation rooms in each camp and a large library, which, unfortunately, has insufficient books and only a few dictionaries—German, English and English–German are needed badly. German was the compulsory language for all of them during their enslavement. I have been to several excellent concerts which are held either in the large tented cinema or the ordinary cinema, both of which are fitted with a stage and drop curtains. The tented building is exceedingly well constructed and, as I told you before, has some kind of air-conditioning plant attached. The wings and curtains are of old-gold damask interwoven with eagle and swastika. To date, I have lacked the courage to souvenir a piece of this material!

On 18th July the first big concert was given by three DPs, Eva Steiner, Soprano (Budapest Opera House); Gerardo Gaudioso, Baritone (S. Carlo, Napoli); and Guiseppe Selmi, Violincello (Radio Roma). Pietro Maggioli was at the piano. Items were from Handel, Chopin, Puccini, Verdi, Liszt and Tosti. The audience, all DPs except for the official parties, was large and most appreciative. Programmes were printed and the whole affair conducted as if it actually had been in the opera house.

On 27th July Yehudi Menuhin visited the camp accompanied

by Benjamin Britten the composer (his latest opera is *Peter Grimes*, I think). They were our guests at the Farm and had dinner with us before the concert. They played for one and a half hours without interval and I do not know which was the more accomplished of the two—both were flawless. They just wore bush shirts and slacks, which blended well with the audience, which was spellbound.

France's National Day, 14th July was celebrated here with Mass and a ceremony held at the present camp cemetery, conducted by the Abbe of the Vatican Mission. I was invited to attend. There are thousands buried here who died since the liberation of Camp 1, those thousands representing almost all nationalities. Long graves hold 200–300 each, side by side; others, more recent, are single. Boards stating such particulars as are known mark the head; some, of course, only have a query; others perhaps only the nationality.

You will remember I told you that all records were destroyed by SS men during the truce and in the early acute days it was impossible to keep accurate records. At this ceremony, Franciscan and St Vincent de Paul nuns who were working in the Hospital placed a bunch of yellow and white wild flowers—the Vatican colours—on each grave. Small white crosses with the French tricolour replaced the original name boards at the head of the French graves. La Marseillaise was played on a gramophone in the broadcasting truck which tours the camp and makes announcements through amplifiers to the people.

Please do not imagine, from the accounts I shall send you of the many social and official activities we attend here, that life for us is one continual round of gaiety—far from it! As it will be quite impossible to write about everything that happens, I shall not dwell on the tragedies with which we come into daily contact or on my own very strenuous professional duties which occupy the major portion of my time. Rather I will endeavour to show you how these recently persecuted souls, whilst emerging from their unutterable past and clutching at a somewhat uncertain future, are making the most of their present security, and how my daily rounds and other nursing activities are punctuated, sometimes to the point of exasperation, with diverse and oft times humorous problems and interruptions inevitably associated with the functioning of an acute and cosmopolitan Hospital such as this.

I think you will agree that it is just as important, in our work of rehabilitation in this community, to encourage and take an active part in the re-awakening interest and psychological adjustments which have to be made as it is to minister to the physical needs of our patients. It is to this end that I shall always make time for my staff and myself to be present whenever possible at any social functions.

Another interesting concert was given by Hungarian DPs in the camp on 16th July. It was also held in the tented cinema and about 700–800 were present. The performers were all DPs and the items were very good. There were piano solos, songs, dances in costume, and a Chinese play, all, of course, in Hungarian. It was compered by the Hungarian Camp Leader and between the items, topical remarks, etc., were translated into English by another Hungarian DP for our benefit. The next day when visiting the Blocks I saw various items of costume which had looked so attractive from the stage. A magnificent head-dress was made of some stiff material decorated with beads, wildflowers, chocolate paper and window, the metal strips dropped by the RAF to upset the German radio and still seen entangled in many fir trees round the camp, reminiscent of Christmas. As a matter of fact, I have been told that the metal was a failure as far as the RAF was concerned but that they continued to use it so that the Germans would think that a similar thing they (the Germans) used was interfering with the RAF's installations! However, it has given much pleasure to the DPs in various ways and the gypsies simply love it.

Spent an hour in the children's clothing store one day recently when the Yugoslav Titos were receiving an outfit prior to returning to their country. Mostly boys seven to thirteen years old, very quiet and well behaved. Those who received one of the twenty remaining brand new suits beamed with pride and pleasure as they fitted them on. These particular children and their parents had not been in concentration camps, but were used as slave labour when the border changed and the Russians drove them into Germany. Most of the clothing was second-hand but all clean and in good order.

I was a guest at a DP's wedding on 21st July. A Polish girl from Camp 1 who had been very ill with typhus had met an ambulance driver of the BRCS who had worked at the evacuation of the Horror Camp. Her name was Toni Sucheka and the groom's Pitrucchi, British, of Italian parentage. In full bridal attire, she looked very attractive. The ceremony was held in the Roman

Catholic 'church', a room in one of the blocks, which was decorated with scarlet rowan-berries, blue lupins and white flowers. A red carper runner with bunches of oak leaves placed at intervals on either side was appropriate. Potted shrubs from the Round House added to the decorations.

The service was short and a Polish DP sang 'Ave Maria' to the accompaniment of a croaky harmonium. The bride's veil had little sprigs of green leaves attached, with a half coronet of the same round the back of her head. I do not know whether this is a national custom or not. She carried a bouquet of a white flower which is plentiful here at present—a cross between white lilac and hydrangea, but I do not know its name. The civil ceremony was combined with the signing of the register. A Polish reception was held first among her friends and then the BRCS gave one in their tented mess. There were Hungarian and Polish cakes and biscuits, sandwiches, and two wedding cakes. The Red Cross in Brussels sent a bottle of champagne and Dr Collis, BRCS, made a speech. There was a box full of presents of all varieties. Streamers of surgical gauze decorated the car in bridal fashion. The happy pair went away for their honeymoon to Copenhagen, I think. You may probably have seen photos of this wedding, which figured in all the British papers.

By the way, the last 200 Tb patients were transferred from the Round House to the Glyn Hughes Hospital on 21st July.

The Post Natal Mothers' home, in the charge of a BRCS Sister, is interesting and houses Hungarians, Poles, Gypsies, German Jews, etc. Some are good mothers, others not so good. Some bedrooms neat and tidy, others not. Mothers come here with their babies when discharged from the Maternity Hospital and frequently bring along their husbands and friends with them for fear of being separated again. They care for their own babies and mix up dreadful-looking pap. Some mothers care for their babies beautifully and it is interesting to see they way they dress them. Many are bound to a pillow—the case of which is made with a loose end which turns up and ties round the baby's waist as a cover—others almost bind them up as bambinos. Dummies, teats and bottles were lying about and flies feasting. Some mothers allow their babies to feed at the breast all day long, and would be aghast at the suggestion of four-hourly intervals! Many are fine babies, others puny, marasmic and premature. A great deal depends on the previous experience of the mother. We will take over the Maternity Hospital and probably this home later, so we may even yet have a miniature King George V Memorial Hospital for Mothers and Babies (recently opened at the Royal Prince Alfred Hospital, Sydney, NSW).

On 24th July I was invited to a reception to meet Field Marshal Lord Chetwode, Head of the BRCS. He arrived with full Field Marshal guard, jeep, motor cycle, Field Marshal's car, one or two other cars, followed by a newly painted truck, with guns bristling and guards fully armed. The Field Marshal told me that UNRRA was invited to come into the British Zone much earlier, but that they stated they were unable to supply the personnel! When I told him how we had been chafing at the bit in London and said that we were given to understand that we had been waiting to be asked by the Military authorities to come in, he told me that had not been necessary and we could have come much sooner!

The other evening, the Gordon Highlanders played the Retreat on one of the Squares at 5 pm and danced a schottische at an open-air dance for the DPs in the evening. The square was decorated with fir trees and shrubs in pots, fairy lights, flags and bunting, and the DPs just loved it. There is so much in which I know you are interested that I could continue indefinitely, but I want to get this away as I have been writing it at intervals for some time now. So many people are writing to me, it is thrilling, but at the moment quite impossible to attempt to answer them. Life is more than hectic but I want you all to keep on writing—letters mean much just now.

Rumours are rife in this community and the administration must be sorely tried at times. Within six hours I heard from official sources that:

1. Ten thousand Wehrmacht wounded and a strong British guard were arriving almost immediately.
2. Russian POWs in large numbers were coming today.
3. Two thousand sick DPs were expected.

So we now wait and wonder just what will turn up!

Chapter 6

MY WORK BEGINS: SUCCESSES AND FRUSTRATIONS

Patients on the balcony of Wards A3 and A4, Glyn Hughes Hospital, Belsen, 1945

Belsen Camp Hospital
13th August 1945

My last letter gave you some idea of the activities of the camp as it was when I arrived. This one will bring you an account of our Mess and things in general.

Until 4th August you will remember I was living as the guest of the Commanding Officer, Military Government HQ, at the German farm. (The British Military Government is in charge of Belsen Camp.) There is also a large garrison of British soldiers stationed here, a necessary precaution in a newly occupied country and a camp of some 20 000 persons of many nationalities, faiths and political parties—in fact a potential volcano.

The surrounding country was pretty when I arrived in early July, as the harvest was ripe and almost ready for reaping. There were some lovely walks, but we womenfolk had been advised not to go out unescorted. Every inch from roadside to horizon is intensively cultivated and each farm has its geese, ducks, chickens, pigs, cows, and horses.

The farm-house in which I lived was a large well-furnished, half-timbered, red brick building, decorated outside with texts and agricultural scenes carved in the black wooden beams, and dated 1925. An attractive weather-vane surmounted the front entrance. A very large kitchen with tiled walls and floor and several sinks combined fuel and electric stove; larders and store-rooms opened directly into a larger barn. Hans the bull reigned supreme over his harem of fourteen: Laura, Annie, Toni, Dolli, Lena, Greta, Olga, Edith, Hilde, Rosa, Ilse, Dea, Isabella and Lore. Each animal had its name-board neatly inscribed. All snored loudly at night!

The flies were terrible, cooked and alive, and as you know some cooks are not always as observant as they should be. There was always plenty of fresh rich creamy milk on the table, but the flies had priority and there were always two or three floating round, which most members of the staff appeared to overlook.

The downstairs rooms were rather inconvenient, as three bedrooms opened one from the other, while the only bathroom was at the extreme end. There was an electric bath-heater, and steam radiators were fitted in all the ground-floor rooms. Tiny observation windows opened from these bedrooms into the barn, where the herd spent the winter. The upstairs bedrooms opened onto a landing which had a connecting door into the loft, so that there was a continual wafting of stable fragrance into the house. The furniture was of the heavy German plush and tasselled variety, the china and glassware quite attractive.

The German Hausfrau, whose husband was a POW, had been evicted and was living with her mother next door. Everything pointed to former prosperity under the Nazi regime. This Hausfrau was instructed by mine host to bring me tea and hot water at 7 am each morning. We always greeted each other cheerfully in German. The local Burgomaster provides the German domestic labour, of which there is no shortage, and so we had German girls to do the housework and my laundry and shoes, and I was moderately comfortable in the German feather bed!

After some weeks the Military Government Officers moved to another mess, and as there were now three UNRRA doctors and myself, the CO invited us to remain. By the way, one of these doctors is Dr Lesley Bidstrup of South Australia.

The Frau's husband returned from the war one day and British armed officials no longer lived there. A stiffening of the pleasant manner was noticed, the standard of housework deteriorated, and the next morning my tea did not appear. On returning that evening we found the best china locked in the side-board! It was interesting to observe the change now that the guns had gone and the German menfolk were coming home.

One night I had a really nerve-racking experience. The others were on an important mission and I was alone until 1.30 am. I had no means of communication whatever with the camp and no transport. I was writing downstairs about 10 pm when I heard the inter-communicating doors from the barn opening. The hinges had dropped and the door scraped the floor. The German cowherd was exploring the upstairs rooms! Although I was unarmed, I knew there was nothing to do but to go up and enquire. I told him to go, and waited until he retreated, then firmly shut the door and went downstairs. Again he came and I went, outwardly so brave, inwardly wondering what on earth would happen next. The same procedure was adopted, but the episode lost its humour when the persistent man returned for the third time! This time, having pushed him out and closed the door, I returned shortly, after noisily opening and shutting the front door, walking heavily on the stairs with the best mannish tread I could muster, and conversing with an imaginary escort as I approached. This ruse was evidently effective for I heard no more of the intruder, but spent an uncomfortable two or three hours in the lighted parlour, which had several large windows but no curtains or blinds, trying to look unconcerned and interested in my work. You can imagine how relieved I was when the party returned.

I was glad when we finally left that farm, for there were now many German Wehrmacht men being released under the British Barley Corn plan to bring the harvest in. Also, a number of Germans near here have been attacked by the DPs recently, one old couple being killed near the farm the week before we left.

Life with UNRRA is not easy! The authorities have provided no cars for the SMO and myself; and as the Glyn Hughes Hospital is at one end of the camp, the Maternity Block the other and the various departments scattered between, the problem of transport is great.

The CO Military Government or one of his Officers always drove us in and out to the farm while they lived there—except on those occasions when I was stranded at the hospital and unable to arrive at HQ meeting place and subsequently missed my lunch! Every other organisation working here is provided with transport and UNRRA is rightly criticised for their neglect. It is a matter of hitch-hiking with any passing vehicle, which is not only embarrassing to me, but often, I am sure, inconvenient to those generously offering assistance.

Repeated appeals brought no result until I had been here four weeks, when after lengthy and confused negotiations on 8th August, a car and an army driver was allotted to me. This, however, was not as good as it sounds for the car had hardly any of its original parts left, and was constantly breaking down at awkward moments. It caught fire once after a German mechanic had repaired it and evidently accidentally left two live wires touching somewhere. It was frequently being borrowed by someone else without my permission, with the result that I was often unable to keep important engagements.

In spite of these difficulties I managed to contact the heads of all the voluntary staff relief societies and the various officials and gained an insight into the functioning of this unique community, as well as spending most of my time each day in the various hospitals. I also went with the Army Quartermaster on a conducted tour to explore the channels through which the food passed from the time it was requisitioned from army stores until the patients received it—and believe me it followed a tortuous passage!

Never will I forget my efforts to find staff accommodation, because the farm was too far away and too small. I had notified the local authorities soon after arrival of my anticipated requirements of UNRRA nurses. These and other UNRRA personnel are expected to total about sixty to seventy, or perhaps more when our organisation finally takes charge of the welfare and other services in the camp as well as the hospital. The Military Government officials, however, wanted a definite date on which the staff were expected, but as we had no idea when this was—nor did anyone else, I fear—the answer just could not be given. We certainly knew that the 81st British General Hospital unit were very anxious for us to take over as soon as possible but that was all.

Time was getting on, and day after day I could get no satisfaction, so in order to have some action, I finally said that I expected my staff any day now. Although wishful thinking, it was near enough to the truth.

Following this, things began to move, even if slowly and sluggishly. First the Camp Commandant offered me the Round House, where you will remember the many thousands of advanced cases of pulmonary Tb and diarrhoea had been nursed under grossly over-crowded, primitive and unhygienic conditions. This building was quite unsuitable for living quarters for a mixed mess, with only the large ballroom, ante-rooms, solaria and cloak-rooms and no baths. It was pervaded with the nauseating odour, which is something one cannot describe but which is common to Belsen, and the last patients had only been evacuated the day before. Even if airing and scrubbing would scientifically be said to make it safe for staff habitation, psychologically it was bad, as death had stalked there so recently. The authorities probably thought I was crazy in not accepting such a palatial abode, but after a detailed inspection my SMO agreed with me on its unsuitability.

The same evening I was told that the recently vacated Children's Hospital was available, but after inspecting it I decided that it was now very dirty and as it had housed many open cases of pulmonary Tb until they died, would require at least two weeks to fumigate, clean and paint.

While the authorities were cogitating over this, I cast my eye on the house in the woods, a large stately white building conveniently situated in a delightful setting of green trees, midway between the camp and the Glyn Hughes Hospital. I imagined how restful and refreshing the grounds would be when my nurses came off duty and thought my worries were at an end.

On investigation, I was told it was occupied by the German owner of the surrounding farms and his wife, who had some members of an Allied agricultural mission and several German Red Cross Nurses living with them. They could not possibly be turned out for the UNRRA nursing staff! Unfortunately, in my enthusiasm, I had focussed the attention of others on this attractive abode, for shortly afterwards we found that the occupants had departed and some Military Government Officials were in residence there.

A barracks building outside the main gates occupied by some of the notorious Hungarian army personnel (who in the terms of the truce were handed over by the Germans to the British, as I have already told you) was the next suggestion. It was exceedingly smelly and dirty, but with soap and water, white-wash, fresh air and the addition of a cook-house and mess would be just passable, failing anything more suitable forthcoming. I was to return in a few days and inspect the results of the Hungarians' efforts at cleaning. Half an hour after my first visit, a deputation of these men (virtual POWs mind you, doing the odd job around the place) strongly objected to the authorities at having to move—so UNRRA again went house-hunting.

As the position was becoming desperate, I suggested we should go under canvas temporarily whilst the recently vacated Children's Hospital building was prepared. After toying with that idea for a week or so, they told me there were too many complications, but that they really had found something good at last!

The something good was a block of four flats near the North Gate in Hoppensted Strasse, which was about to fall vacant on Wednesday 1st August, then cleaned on 2nd August and handed over to me on 3rd August. I was so relieved to think we would have a spick and span apartment to commence with.

The advance party of my nursing staff was expected on the 3rd or 4th August, and I was to take over the entire hospital, including the maternity unit some distance away, on the 6th. It would mean pretty hard going, but could be managed, and I slept well that night as my relief was so great at finally finding a home for my staff. As nothing ever goes as anticipated here I was not surprised the next morning to hear that the Army evacuation had been postponed for twenty-four hours!

During my hitch-hike on these house-hunting peregrinations, I spent any spare time arranging details with the various officials, engaging DP cooks, and German cleaners, checking up on furniture, china and cutlery, and ordinary rations. Planning meal and duty hours, endeavouring to requisition the bus used to take Army sisters to and from duty for our use when they left, drawing up a bus timetable, allotting rooms, scrounging cleaning materials, which strangely are not on issue for our mess. All this, plus a thousand other things, kept me occupied—especially the hitch-hiking from one end of the camp to the other. My SMO could not understand why all these matters could not wait until my staff arrived! In the midst of all this, on 31st July, the UNRRA Medical Director of British Zone sent a request that the two medical officers and I prepare an inventory of all deficiencies in equipment in the entire hospital by 1st August. Fortunately I had noticed many of the deficiencies during my rounds and we duly completed a staggering list after sitting up all night, and sent it off poste-haste to local HQ, quietly hoping it would give them as bad a headache as it had given us.

During my peregrinations I was invited to take several odd cups of tea with the OC of the RASC Unit and accepted, hoping to entice him to at least complete the cleaning of the top flats to enable us to get on with the job.[1] I was notified that these would be vacated at 10.30 am on 3rd August and I thought all I had to do was to arrange the furniture and the culinary department.

Alas! They just walked out and overlooked the cleaning, and having been well installed and very busy since Belsen's early days,

---

1 RASC is believed to be an abbreviation for The Royal Army Sanitary Corp.

you can imagine things were in a frightful mess. Rubbish cluttered every room and junk of all varieties abounded. I first had to locate and send an SOS to the accommodation officer who sent nine Hungarian soldiers, and to the Sergeant in charge of labour who offered six German cleaning women (and, by the way, twelve arrived). I personally went to the Deputy Assistant Director Ordnance Store to beg a few scrubbing brushes, buckets, brooms and rags, to which I was informed I was not entitled. I also got one small precious bar of soap. The BRCS women in charge of these stores were most sympathetic and helpful and lent me whatever they could, and more than I asked for, so long as I signed for them to guarantee their return.

Then the fun began! I turned out masses of useless, broken down furniture and had to find transport to remove it—lorry loads of it. The day was spent patrolling and driving the dirty, lazy Hungarian creatures and the German women, for they either sat or lay on the couches the minute my back was turned. The men, under pressure, moved the furniture, swept and scrubbed and I set women to cleaning the windows, wardrobes, drawers and bathrooms. If ever there was an example of passive resistance it was seen that day, and I suppose I would have done the same. You see, I had no gun, which is the language they understood. One or two women worked fairly well, but all were exceedingly slow. It was exhausting, but at least the outer grime was removed and the furniture cleaned and rearranged. I was instructed that they all had to cease work at 5 pm so I continued alone—exhausted and exasperated. That night I sat up until well after midnight waiting for the Medical Director and Chief Nurse of the British Zone, who were expected but who did not arrive.

The morning of 4th August brought forth six new German women and a fresh party of twelve Hungarian soldiers, but the RASC did not leave the lower flats until 11 am. What a mess—some rooms had been offices and they looked chaotic when the army gear had been removed. The OC generously left us about one dozen bottles of wine and a quantity of tea, sugar, etc. Between his leaving at 11 am and my walking downstairs a few minutes later, all the wine had completely vanished and nine of the Hungarians were in the kitchen, each with two enormous thick slices of bread inches deep with butter or margarine with mountains of marmalade on top! I literally drove them out, and found a British Tommy who came to my assistance. These lazy creatures only seemed to move when one shouted and banged or stamped one's foot like a sergeant major. I chuckled to think what you would say if you could have seen me then.

I walked up and down all day long. Three of the four electric stoves would not work, door handles were broken, keys missing, doors would not open, electric fittings were without globes or out of order, chains would not pull, baths and basins were without plugs, panes of glass in windows and balcony doors were missing or smashed—in fact *alles kaput* is a term which expresses much and is understood by all. After ringing on and off for one hour on the RASC phone across the road, I contacted the Garrison engineer, who finally sent me a plumber, electrician, locksmith, glazier and carpenter—all Germans. The language difficulty was soon overcome, for everything was *kaput* or *alles kaput* with a vast and embracing wave of one's hands.

Much patrolling was necessary here also, for these German workmen were also quite ready to sit down and peruse the latest illustrated London magazines they found, rather than attend to the repairs. Day after day they came—new basins to replace those with the bottoms out, new lights to be fitted, locks to be repaired, and so on. What a life! It really was fun and I thoroughly enjoyed getting order out of chaos, but how my feet ached at night.

In the middle of all this the officials who had been expected the previous evening arrived for lunch, bringing with them the first five nurses, but no housekeeper. The nurses were more than appreciated but little did they suspect what was ahead of them. The Heads would have been more warmly welcomed a week or so later, but we managed to feed them all at the farm, and they did not stay long, so all was well. Alas! Whilst I was greeting the party, the precious soap and scrubbing brushes vanished, ne'er to be seen again.

I did not realise it was so late and as I must get some sleep I shall have to continue this later in the week.

Continued 18th August 1945

Our Hungarian cook Mischa, and his two assistants Lajor and Ferenc, who had previously worked at the Children's Hospital, miraculously gave us all a hot dinner in our new mess at 7 pm that evening. I had ordered, and assisted by our two doctors collected, double rations for the weekend but gypsies are opportunists and must have seen them arrive, for at 7 am on Saturday they stole the whole lot under our very noses. Mili, our Czech cook-supervisor who had just arrived, chased one who had the spoils in a large bag or bags, which had apparently contained bandages and surgical dressings, now hastily discharged in the garden when more interesting and satisfying goods were offering! Mili, in her dressing gown, caught the intruder down the road, but whilst awaiting assistance from a stalwart army lad whom she had called, a gypsy colleague hovering nearby gathered the takings and vanished. I do wish I could have seen that episode—we had to laugh, serious as it was. However, the Army authorities came to our rescue as usual and provided more rations.

The second block of flats had yet to be attacked and still no housekeeper had appeared on the scene. These flats further up Hoppenstedt Strasse were occupied by DPs who had volunteered to work in the camp laundry. They were very comfortable, for when the Germans were evicted or hastily fled at the time the British came, they had left everything behind. So that the DPs would not remove the contents when other accommodation was found for them, they were given no warning. An army truck just came to the door one morning and they were told they were going to new quarters and were driven away, taking only their personal belongings. That was a week or two before the flats were handed over to me, so you can imagine the state they were in when I got the keys and entered. There were masses of quite good but heavy-type German furniture, pianos, stale food, mice, old mattresses, blankets and much dirt. The kitchens were awful. It looked hopeless. This time I fortunately had the five nurses to help me supervise: Miss Szloch (USA), Miss Vanderwell (Canada), Miss Stenhouse (Scotland), Misses Sohr and Willaert (Belgium), an excellent and most willing team.

Since my visit the day before, the place had been broken into, all the keys I had carefully fitted to each door had been removed, and bedside lamps, bedsteads, a piano, china and cutlery taken. This was reported to the appropriate authorities, but we were unable to follow it up as it was hinted that the goods had been removed by some enterprising British Officers, who evidently had an eye to their own comfort and who had first refusal, as it were.

You see, a new contagious disease has been introduced into Europe, as a result of the Nazi new order. Now, if you covet your neighbours' possessions, you just liberate them for your own purpose. Some of those DPs who during their imprisonment or slavery were forced to resort to this means of acquiring things of vital necessity for themselves will find it exceedingly difficult and will need assistance to live normally in a normal community again. Then it was every man for himself and now this still prevails in many cases. They are taking advantage of the fine weather and it is a common sight to see groups of men, women and children helping themselves to large quantities of potatoes and vegetables from the German farms—reparations, did you say?

The roads round Dageford are lined with apple trees which they are also stripping. They look such hard little apples too, but the DPs tummies have had to cope with much more difficult things than fresh green German apples, which they appear to relish.

Another term which has been coined here is heard in reply to an enquiry as to where so-and-so got that pretty blouse, or smart handbag. One may be told, 'Oh, eet ees organise madame,' with an entrancing smile, or the answer may be just, '*Klipsi, klipsi*,' with a shrug of the shoulders and a knowing wink of the eye. They are perfectly honest about it all and consider they are entitled to take any German goods they want—perhaps they are.

Joined by three more nurses the next morning—Miss Barstch (Canada), Miss Richards (England), Miss Gillet (France)—we forged ahead, driving our team of workers, and after a few days had the place in fairly good order, if not a home from home. Freda, a Hungarian gypsy about four years old, a patient from the hospital, helped me to label the keys of every cupboard I could find. We now have our Mess Committee and will be quite comfortable in the winter with our chip heaters and enormous radiators, if only we have the chips and the coal.

Five more nurses arrived by 12th August, and one who had been sent temporarily was withdrawn that day. Miss Doris Delaney from New South Wales arrived on the 14th, but my efforts to procure a housekeeper have only brought forth an assurance from UNRRA local HQ that she is expected to arrive on 27th August, unfortunately just about six weeks too late! With twelve UNRRA nurses, after an overlap of two days on 13th August, I officially took over the Hospital from the British Matron and her staff of twenty-two, which she told me was inadequate for all the supervision necessary. You can imagine the administration is very difficult in these early days under such abnormal conditions and with such a small UNRRA staff.

The DP Polish waiter in our mess was once employed in an Officers' Club in Poland, and DP girls of various nationalities have volunteered to do our housework. Four Hungarian girls came first, remained one day and did not return, as they did not care for general domestic work. The next day four more came, but did not remain long either. I think this is partly due to their newly found independence and partly to the fact that they are not yet able to apply themselves to continuous work after their severe illnesses and terrible experiences.

Piri, a pretty little Romanian Jewess, looks after me, irons and mends beautifully and is very neat and tidy. Her friend Irma Schlomer, a Hungarian, is my clerk-interpreter, speaks French, English and German fluently and is an efficient typist in those languages. She tells me that before the war her father owned a large Sanatorium in Berlin, but she does not know where he is now. Her mother died in the Horror Camp just before liberation. She is still very weak from typhus, tires easily and is dazed from her recent experiences, but seems happy to be working again and certainly is a great help to me. Having no housekeeper in the Mess, nor messing officer in the hospital to date, I'm head serang of all. Having no Welfare Officer I've taken over that Department also. The Army Welfare Officer left me practically no stocks and as all male patients receive three and females one cigarette daily and eight sweets each, I feared there would be a revolution if I failed to produce those priceless commodities—especially on the first day UNRRA took over.

However, after an exhausting search among camp authorities I collected 3000 face-saving cigarettes, which unfortunately will not last long, particularly as the eight or nine DP girls who assist with the distribution get ten each as well.

Staff outside A1 Ward, Glyn Hughes Hospital, Belsen, 1945: from left to right, Miss Willaert (Belgian nurse), Miss Doherty, Miss Szloch (American nurse), Mrs Jackson (English Messing Officer)

Belsen
25th August 1945

I try to add a little to my letters every day but because of the many distractions and frequent interruptions I am afraid you will find some of them rather disjointed—however, from all accounts you are interested in the news I give you, so I will continue to jot down a day-to-day story, as it were.

When the army handed over to me they told me I had 135 German Nurses—but I could only find 111. Next day a racket began when nearly every one of them applied for two days' leave in Hamburg, while some, I fear, took the leave without applying! It's one thing knowing what you should have and quite another knowing where they are.

I set out to account for them all. It has taken my Canadian assistant Miss Louise Bartsch and me two weeks to complete the list. I have a German Matron, Frau Ella Bach, who is responsible to me for the German Nursing staff, and a Latvian Matron, Erika Sedmalis, in charge of the nurses from the Baltic States. Not one list the German Matron gave me tallied with any other—we finally, with swimming heads, found we had 131, including the Matron, and have card indexed each one.

The Hamburg tour was quickly quelled and a system of leave instituted. I have given them one day off per week and three hours per day, and have worked out a system of exchange because some of them have been here since liberation and really do look rather tired. Others wish to return to their ex-POW husbands who have been demobilised, and some say they are to be married. One nurse applied for discharge on the latter grounds, and as I had seen her wearing a wedding ring on her left hand, I wondered. On enquiring I found in Germany the ring is worn on the left hand for betrothal and is placed on the right hand during the wedding ceremony.

One day recently I happened to return to the Hospital in the lunch hour and found two large white German Red Cross buses and a trailer disgorging nurses—sixty of them!

I sent for the German Matron and found that the German Department of Public Health in Hamburg had sent them for exchange and were taking a similar number back. I thought differently and hastily found our SMO. We decided that could not be allowed on principle. After an interview with the high-handed German Medical Officer who had travelled with them, he was instructed to take them all back to Hamburg and make an official request for exchange which would be considered by us.

Our Latvian nurses, who previously had led me to believe that they had come voluntarily during the war to work in the German hospitals, changed their mind the other day; perhaps it was because they saw the DPs in Hospital receiving special clothing issues, or perhaps we had misunderstood them before. However, after a security officer had interviewed the Latvian Matron, they signed a statement, which I am now satisfied is the truth, to the effect that they had been forced by the Germans when they occupied Latvia to work first in German Hospitals there, and then to move into Germany to work in Military Hospitals. Having established themselves as DPs they now receive the special issue.

The Latvian Matron reports to me every morning at 10 am after I have seen the German Matron; she doesn't speak a word of English, and you all know what my Latvian is like! She brings one of her staff who speaks a little English, and so we get along with that, punctuated with smiles, bows and gestures and assisted by my interpreter when necessary. The Latvian nurses' work is not terribly outstanding and as they say they do not like working with the Germans we are constantly having friction. Five are trained, the others are Nurse Helps, as they are called.

The German nursing set up is unlike anything we know. Before the war there were three main nursing organisations in Germany, the Evangelical Deaconesses, the Catholic Nuns and the German Red Cross sisterhood, all of which were attached to their mother-houses. When the Nazis were not as successful as they hoped in bringing these bodies entirely into their scheme, two new organisations were formed—the National Socialist and the Free Nurses, both of which were highly political and not responsible to the mother-houses. All five bodies were combined under one Nazi National Organisation.

The Midwife or *Hebamme* played an important part in the Nazi health services and they were also compelled to belong to the Nazi organisation. There were also trained children's nurses and public health nurses, both of whom underwent a special training, and, of course, district and private duty nurses, all of whom came under Nazi control.

It has been established that the Nazis considered the nursing profession and the German Red Cross two of their most powerful weapons for the dissemination of their vile doctrines, as these people came into such close contact with a large number of the community and thus offered unusual opportunities for spreading political propaganda.

The Nazi nursing text book, a copy of which I managed to procure from the Public Health Library in Hamburg, was written by a doctor in the Ministry in Berlin. A large portion is devoted to the Nazi racial and biological doctrines, which as you know were, in general, anti-Semitism, legal abortion, compulsory sterilisation of the mentally defective, liquidation of the mentally and physically unfit, and above all the superiority of the *Herrenvolk* or German Master Race.

The length of training for general nurses in pre-war Germany was two and a half to three years, but during the recent war this was reduced to two years for Red Cross Nurses and one and a half years for the others, and included a good deal of training in domestic work and Nazi politics.

Since 1933, when Adolf Hitler became Chancellor, a considerable amount of time during the training was devoted to the study of Nazi teachings—the young nurses have known nothing but the Master Race doctrine. They were trained to accept the shocking treatment meted out to foreign slave workers imported by the Nazis as part of this policy. Their bedside nursing on the whole is poor, but as we organise ward duties we hope to improve that. The older ones who trained in pre-Nazi days seem a little better, but with a few exceptions I would say from my observations that the general standard is well below our own.

Evacuation of patients has been carried out at a rapid pace. Hospital train after train has left, packed with mostly lying patients, many accompanied by relatives, for the policy is to keep families together as much as possible. I went to see a train depart for Sweden the other evening and the OC took me right through. There were 320 patients, many of them thin, ill and unhappy-looking, others brighter and more cheerful. It was 6 pm and they were having their tea, which consisted of dark rye bread and butter and a tin of peculiar, greyish-looking fish floating in a more peculiar murky-looking liquid, which they appeared to relish. Some of the patients looked very ill—the doctor did not expect one girl to reach her destination, but wanted to give her the satisfaction of leaving Belsen.

These people, tasting real freedom once more, would be convoyed in that train as far as Lübeck, where the Swedish Red Cross would take them over, medically examine, re-delouse and re-clothe them before commencing the remainder of the journey. Sweden has undertaken to look after some thousands of these people for six months or so. Perhaps their ball-bearing conscience pricks them at last.

I love to visit the camp squares on the occasions when a transport is leaving with happy, well-fed, warmly clad repatriates. Army trucks and lorries which convey them are stocked with food and decorated with garlands, branches and national flags. Sometimes a band plays as they are being comfortably seated with their worldly possessions around them, and the Military Government and voluntary organisation officials farewell them. With the singing of National Anthems and much hand waving they leave us to start life once again in their own country as the long convey passes out of sight.

The UNRRA staff have been arriving in dribs and drabs and at present we have thirty-three members in the mess, including thirteen nurses, representing many nationalities—Czech, Polish, English, Scottish, Northern Irish, French, Dutch, Canadian, Belgian, Danish and Australian—a truly international unit.

I wonder how Australia celebrated the cessation of hostilities with Japan, and what the Son of Heaven will do now? When I told Mischa the war with Japan was over he nearly threw his arms round my neck and kissed me!

We had a special dinner of international dishes on 16th August and later went to the Officers' Club to hear our King's speech, which came over very clearly. This very beautiful club was built by a Hamburg coffee merchant and was, until taken over by the British, Kramer's residence I believe.

From what I have seen already of the European chaos, I think the winning of the peace will be even more difficult than winning the war. It's all frightfully interesting here, but an enormous undertaking, which can only be successful if UNRRA gives us sufficient staff. I have stressed this in reports and have been told by our local HQ that I can have about six more nurses than I have requested, but somehow, after the way we began, I feel doubtful as to whether they will materialise.

PS: The 3000 Russians from the Ruhr who invaded this Camp during the last three days lost no time in erecting enormous pictures of Stalin, Lenin, and someone called Zacov, decorated with suitable inscriptions over the main door of each block in the squares. Red stars and the hammer and sickle are displayed everywhere, and next door are 4000 Poles! The Russians are being X-rayed in the Glyn Hughes; they appear stocky, husky creatures but are all suspected of having pulmonary Tb. Those well enough wander round and nearly always carry a flower. They are already very interested in the Glyn Hughes and we jokingly say they will be in occupation before we know where we are.

I have instituted weekly conferences with the UNRRA nurses, at which they can bring up any matter for discussion without previous notice. This is one reason, I think, why I have always had their wholehearted co-operation. In this way we have been able to introduce some measure of uniformity of administration and to rectify quite a number of unsatisfactory matters, at the same time strengthening our team work.

Constructive criticism and suggestions are welcomed and many valuable contributions have been made. I feel that this is also the reason why we are such a happy group in spite of all our difficulties and frustrations. All are united in their efforts to do their utmost for these unfortunate people, our patients.

Letter from German nurse
undated
Hamburg

Dear Miss Doherty,
How few weeks have passed since I left Belsen. I have been there for four months, from May to September 1945. I have been ordered, together with a number of sisters from Hamburg, to a duty 'not far from Hamburg' at patients who were somewhat weak.

We were told that we had to stay outside for a fortnight or three weeks. We were told to take with us the storm baggage, that means the things we had taken with us to the cellar during the war when the bombs arrived. We didn't know if we had to be on duty by nursing civil patients who had suffered from the terror or soldiers or what else. We started from Hamburg to do our best and to help where help was necessary. Our first experience when we arrived at Belsen was this: we learned to understand why we are the best hated nation in the world. Indeed terrible things happened in the concentration camps, especially during the last months of the war. More than once the English asked us, 'How is it possible that you didn't know this?' 'Why didn't your own people stop those awful things?' It may be that the people in the concentration camp are not angels, but the Germans treated the poor people in a manner that isn't human-like at all and it was very sorrowful and not easy for us to bear this blame.

The first days all were crying, 'Sister, *Schwester*, *Suchwerb ra*, Fräulein, Madam, basin *pfanne*, *Schüssel*, *Einner*, *Schole*, hunger, drink, *dunk*, *dunk*.' When I was going round with my little table to make the dressings (nearly all the patients had wounds, sometimes bad phlegmone and sometimes abscesses or furuncle. And sometimes only a little) the patients were crying, '*Schwester*, operation, *Schwester*, medication!' 'Do my dressing first.' 'No, mine first,' called the other. I told them that I would not be off duty and leave the ward till all would be cared of and all would be satisfied. Few days later the patients began to respect us and they were thankful.

To the English doctor the patients said 'Sister good, Sister Puma.' The doctor was very glad to hear this and he said to me, 'From which hospital you and your sisters all coming? I see you have learned to work very hard and in a good way. I can explain you this and that and I see the sisters are doing their best to make everything alright. I thank you very much. If there is anything difficult you can tell me and I will help you.'

The recognition of the German Sisters carried out by the English doctor seemed like a bit of sunshine in the dark after sorrowful days. By the time our Sisters arrived and the patients were no more so very weak and sick. Then, the Sweden start began, that means the doctor asked the patients if they would like to make a tour of Sweden and to stay there for few months in order to become healthy. Sometimes it was somewhat difficult to explain to the patients that it would be the best for them to go to Sweden. After a Sweden start the hospital had a lot of empty beds, but only for a few hours one day. Then other people arrived. These patients were not only from Belsen but other parts of Germany.

When I had been at Belsen for three months my health was not the best and I felt very weak. I was ordered to be some days off duty. But I was not what you'd call sick, the pain was inside my head. I wanted to help the poor people, but was aware we could do but little. I loved to spare some time for the patients not only for dressings and medications. The patients were very glad and thankful when I had some time for them to talk. First I had to listen to what they have suffered and I told them, 'Don't always remember the terrible and awful time and look forward. How it will be better for you!' It's no good for your health to think about the very sorry things always and only. For nobody it's possible to think about sorry things every day and every night. I have done it at Belsen. These were my thoughts. We have lost the war, and our country. There are only Germans and no Germany in this war. The most German soldiers who have suffered from the war for six long years lost their homes, their family, their profession. But the worst of all is the concentration camp. There we lost our honour! A good German he cannot bear life without honour! It doesn't matter that we didn't know what happened in the concentration camp, we have to bear the blame!

All that we want from other countries with time is this—neither pity or kindness but believing that not all Germans are bad and terrible and that the German spirit is technical as well, as in arts, music, and so on, and is still our life.

(Signed)
Schwester Lottie Burns[1]

1 Lottie Burns was a member of the German nursing staff at Belsen from May to September 1945.

Belsen
29th August 1945

Life is rather hectic and very trying at present. Today it reached its peak! Among a thousand other things this is what happened. I was standing at the Deputy SMO's office window waiting for him to return, when a harassed-looking Tommy from the Guard Room at our main Hospital gate (we have six gates, twenty-eight holes in the fence and one guard room) came up and asked if there was a responsible UNRRA officer about. Thinking I might possibly come under that heading I asked if I could help him.

'Well,' said he, 'there are 200–300 Italians at the gate demanding entry.' I enquired if they were patients, for it has not been an uncommon occurrence in the past for fifty or more to arrive practically unannounced, regardless of whether we have any empty beds or not. 'No,' said he, 'they are milling around waving flags and things.' I told him to keep them outside until I made some enquiries. Thinking the SMO might know something about it I popped my head in his office door to find two French nuns, an Italian liaison officer and a couple of interpreters, all looking very solemn and anxious. I found they had come to hold Requiem Mass for an Italian patient who died yesterday and that when the SMO had taken them to the Mortuary to collect the body it had vanished! The 300 Italians had come to the funeral.

I hastily withdrew and sent an SOS to some of my staff to assist in the search for the body, provided a table and clean sheet for the nuns, and took them over to the Mortuary to be sure they had everything they wanted to set up an altar and then hopefully watch for the return of the corpse.

After some time and an exhaustive search, it was revealed that another group of Italians, having purloined the body, were supervising the burial in the Camp Cemetery! Fortunately there was time to restore the body and hold the service as arranged at first, and all was well.

Returning to the hospital I found my staff had been instructed by a young woman doctor to commence moving the beds in this 560-bed hospital to suit her reclassification. An extensive classification and spacing of beds had only been carried out ten days ago, just after we took over from the Army, who had also made a rough classification before handing over to us, and we prayed we'd never move another bed. Apart from the work entailed, it is very upsetting to our patients to be constantly moved from their friends and relatives, and the UNRRA nurses say they just couldn't cope with another big upheaval.

Having cleared that little matter up, or rather deferred the evil moment, I heard that 120 Poles were to be admitted, and found there was not an empty bed in the place. This meant hasty improvisation. Just as I was arranging this, a security officer from Military Government called at my office to interview the Latvian Matron again as to how, when, where and why she and her nurses first came to Belsen. During this interview a number of patients with gastro-enteritis were admitted to the new Maternity Wing, to which we had intended to admit our first obstetric cases tomorrow!

I spent a good part of the afternoon with the German Matron discussing each one of her staff of 130 nurses, deciding who should go on leave to Hamburg, who should be exchanged, and how many we required in each ward when the rearrangement of patients, which we had managed with great difficulty to defer today, takes place.

Emerging from this I was told that a case of Fleck fever (Typhus) had been admitted and no one could find the DDT powder or gun for dusting. Fresh supplies were ordered three weeks ago, but we had a small amount on hand which was supposed to be kept in a certain place known to all.

An admission of this kind involves, among a host of other things, contacting camp officials to investigate from where the patient came and ensuring that every precaution is taken to prevent an epidemic.

Talking of DDT, the German nurses seem to have a passion for scrubbing walls and woodwork in preference to nursing the patients. We found bed bugs in the wooden panelling of one of our wards today, so when the DDT powder was run to earth, a nurse was instructed to use it. An hour later we found another nurse washing it all off! So had to commence all over again. Accidental, did you say?

On my way back from the isolation wards a German *Oberschwester* (Senior Sister) stopped me to say that there was no black tea, carrot juice or glucose for the gastro babies, and no diet for the gall bladders. The German doctors have some treatments which seem strange to us. This shortage of food for the babies was an ill wind, for it gave me the opportunity to persuade them to use the standard treatment of the Children's Hospital (Royal Alexandria Hospital for Children) in Sydney. The babies are dehydrated and are not progressing and now I hope for some improvement.

A patient reported one of the German nurses today, because she (the patient) had been forced to work as a slave for the nurse's sister, who was an ardent Nazi, and she recognised the nurse as also being an active party member. This little episode took up quite a lot of time and means another enquiry, later, probably followed by the arrest of the nurse.

At lunch time there was a riot in one of the wards! The cooks had put all the vegetables in the stew. Plates were flying and the patients were out of bed, milling round, by the time I arrived on the scene. They refused to eat the stew, which they said was the same as the Germans gave them in the Concentration Camps. They are just like children but disturbances like this could lead to much trouble. We finally got them all peaceably back to bed after a good deal of argument, many protests, much cajoling and an issue of bread and cheese from the kitchen. Then followed a conference with the UNRRA nurse in charge of the ward and the messing officer, at which it was decided that in future the vegetables will be served separately.

After all these weeks I am still battling, bargaining and beseeching for transport that will move. I heard today that an army driver by the name of Saint had been looking for me all the morning. On contacting him I found he was without a car, and as my first one is *kaput,* I am now wondering whether a rickshaw will appear, or whether we shall both mount shank's pony or perhaps grow wings.

The water and electricity was off in the hospital and the mess at 7.30 am today without warning. It is becoming a habit for breakdowns to occur now, owing to a shortage of coal and overloading of the power. I have begged the QM to find some wood-burning stoves which could be put outside each block to provide hot water in these emergencies. It is also terribly difficult in the kitchen, where all the cooking is done by either steam or electricity. Certainly we have one or two fuel boilers outside the kitchen which are a great help but quite inadequate for the large amount of cooking which is necessary. The result is that we cannot always serve the hot meals we would like.

The day before yesterday the housekeeper for our mess finally arrived at lunch time, accompanied by her dog. She was openly annoyed at being sent to Belsen. The SMO, before everyone, told her she could make up her mind to send the dog back or go herself. The tension was terrible because we had been awaiting her arrival so anxiously and needed her so badly.

This tactful welcome caused her to leave the table hastily. I hurriedly followed, endeavouring to persuade her to return; offered her any room in the house and found a corner in the garage for the temporary abode of the dog, collected some fresh water for it as appeasement, and suggested the Hungarians might make a kennel, etc., etc. The hound is on her balcony tonight, she is still with us and so life goes on!

I have been rather worried about the German nurses' quarters lately and so decided to do full rounds again today. One hundred and thirty-five live in an unlined attic over one of the hospital blocks and they only have two enamel wash-basins and water from a fire hydrant. The only light and air enters from a few small and very thick frosted-glass windows in the tiled roof. They could not be more than twelve inches square.

Something will have to be done before the winter, and they will have to have some form of heating or we will have an epidemic or they will be unable to work. I found they are well supplied with bed linen in spite of the shortage in the wards, and have instructed the Matron that they cannot have sheets while we are unable to change the patients' beds.

We go on merrily admitting and discharging patients, and patients go on busily admitting and discharging themselves, so life is never dull. They still wander away at night and perhaps return the next day or a few days later, quite cheerfully having tasted this freedom once more. It is when one's sick Tb patient takes it into his head to spend the night in the fields that one begins to worry. Especially if it is damp, but they don't appear to be any the worse for their experience when they return.

Talking of our Tb patients, a few extracts from ward Sisters' fairly recent reports will illustrate what I have told you.

> The following two patients (open Tb) were not available for examination as they were out walking. Dajtilo Borjik (open Tb)

> patient demanded the doctor on return to bed. Had been to the Lager all the afternoon until late at night, helping his friends to move beds as Russian POW Tb patients were expected and the blocks were being cleared. Boris Trocksch (Tb) patient spit blood, given Morphia gr. 1/4 at midday. Walked up and down the corridor all the afternoon. Six women from Ward A1 (surgical) and patients from Ward A3 (male Tb) were visiting in this ward at all hours of the night and we had quite a time to get them back to their respective beds. Albino Bordinskyl (Tb) bed-rest patient, found fully dressed returning from a visit to the camp. Bernislava Koscherowska (female) out all night, not yet returned, 4 am. Anna Stephanoska (female, open Tb) insisted on attending the dance in the concert hall this afternoon, as she wished to dance with her very dear friend from A2 (male surgical).

Now I ask you, what *would* you do?

Thought I would wander over and inspect the mattress disinfector today, where a German is in charge. It had been raining all night and you can imagine my amazement when I saw dozens and dozens of sections of mattresses strewn on the wet ground. As there was neither coal, water nor electricity, the silly man had put the half autoclaved ones to dry off and had added those awaiting sterilisation—hoping we would have some sunshine, I suppose! Or was he so silly? I took the SMO to see this devastating scene and then we had them all moved to the attics—but they will take a long time to dry thoroughly.

A little time ago, I arranged to have one of the sewing machines transferred from the hospital to our mess when transport was available. At lunch today we heard that the driver, finding the flats locked, took the machine temporarily to a garage next door occupied by some British Army men. He was about to unload it and ask them to deliver it later when two German cleaning women from the liaison officers' flats opposite came out and said the machine had been lent to them for five days! They were in the process of taking possession when an UNRRA nurse appeared and, knowing the machine was expected, demanded its immediate surrender.

The curfew outside my window has just wailed so it must be 10.50 pm. It is an old German air raid signal and will emit its second warning shriek at 11 pm, after which we will hope to settle down, if not to sleep.

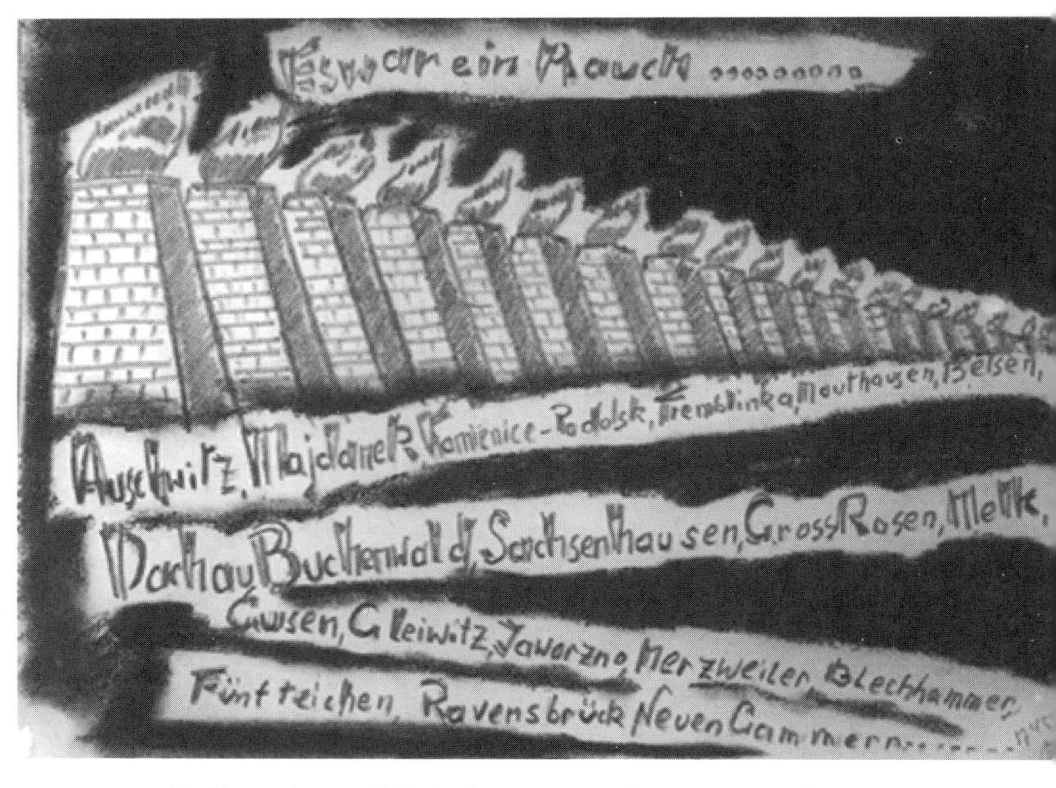

F. Tannenbaum, 'Life in Concentration Camp' series, Belsen, 1945

Belsen
5th September 1945

My first day off for two months—I stayed in bed till 3 pm and now, completely refreshed, I'm on my little balcony with forest all round. The berries and rosehips are scarlet, indicative of a sharp winter, but the sun is shining at present, although there is a distinct nip in the air. The sections of paling fences, which are erected to prevent the snow drifting across the roads, are being piled in readiness. This winter our DPs will have adequate food, shelter and clothing, if insufficient heating. For some it will be the first winter out of prison for ten or eleven years and we are anxious to make it as comfortable and happy as possible.

I shall again endeavour to give you some news of interest from this community, which is still teeming with life, activity and problems. It is such a place of contradictions that sometimes I wonder if the world will ever be sane again.

I have sixteen UNRRA nurses on my staff today, including myself, but that won't last long as they are being changed so frequently. The more we set right in the hospital, the more there appears to be to do, it is just endless and sometimes hopeless to achieve anything. Take the question of linen—when we came, all the linen for the Camp Hospitals and other Departments was sent from the Army laundry to Woolworths and distributed to those units requiring it. One just went as often as one liked and asked for what was wanted. First come first served and no questions asked, sort of thing. Well, that was alright as long as the supply lasted, but, as I have told you, when one has been without clothes for five to six years or more, what does a sheet or two and German ones at that, matter? And so the supply dwindled and the source dried up. When we took over the hospital I found there was practically nothing in the hospital linen room and not much more on the beds. The linen room was in the charge of a British Sergeant and there was a constant stream of German Nurses (and others) supposedly exchanging article for article, but no record was kept. Did I tell you that in one month 10 000 sheets were missing? And that was soon after we took over and found the cupboard practically bare.

I put a Sister in charge of the linen and we removed two of the three Hungarian soldiers who lounged there and engaged a Russian girl, who has lived in Germany many years. We drew up linen requisition slips which now come to my office every morning. We have barricaded the door and keep records. Our shelves are not so bare, although there are still some leakages and we can't be there all the time. We managed to get a supply of new sheets recently and have marked them in the centre and at both ends with some marking ink from London. We've had all mending sorted but have no thread and only one needle. The Polish DP tailor we engaged to do the repairs absconded the next day with an electric iron belonging to our Polish QM! Then we found four machines, a German sewing woman and a reel of thread. The seamstress broke the one needle and hasn't been seen since! Our third attempt is now being made. This week we found we had lost 1000 hand towels since the last count and are sure it happens in the laundry. I have just received dozens of long cotton underpants, which at a pinch would do as pyjamas, and some yellow flannelette bed jackets which will do for the Maternity ward.

The blankets are another anxiety for they are a source of a brisk tailoring industry, as well as smart berets, shopping bags and forage caps. Winter is ahead and we know coal will be short so we are trying to hoard all blankets. Our QM found some on his shopping expedition last week, so we have a nice roomful now and soon will see that each patient again has three on his bed. We have decided to note the number of sheets and blankets on the board bearing the patient's name and nationality, which is at the head of each bed, and see if that works. The Continentals do not as a rule tuck the upper bed-clothes in, but we are going to encourage them to do so—it would be warmer and less easy for friends to slip away with a blanket at visiting times!

Did I tell you 20 000 DPs are expected to be in the Camp for the winter? How they will exist cooped up in the intense cold with a shortage of fuel and nothing to do I cannot imagine. Of course there are always the trees in the forests which can be chopped down to yield firewood, I suppose.

Warm clothes are in very short supply, consequently our blankets will be in greater demand as time goes on, and *Klipsi, Klipsi* is the order of the day. On doing rounds the other day one of my male patients was happily sitting on his bed with scissors and thread and a smart pair of half made pantaloons in dark grey blanket, which he proudly displayed. What could one do but admire such innocent enterprise?

We were given twenty-five cases of US layettes a couple of weeks ago. I was in my element. We had them conveyed into an empty room and got the Hungarians up to open six only, while we stood there. We removed the contents from two and did not open the packing of the others. I personally locked the door and window. Next day all six cases had been opened and eight lovely US blankets were missing. They were at the bottom and the Hungarians were the only ones who knew they were there. They may, of course, have been pilfered during packing in the USA!

Please don't think all the DPs are really dishonest, but it is just the reaction after so much deprivation and concentration camp life. The problem is that some, having lost their sense of values, may spend their lives in and out of trouble when they move to their own or other countries.

Two patients with diphtheria awaiting transfer to the infectious ward went out for a walk with a crowd of their girlfriends yesterday and it was several hours before they were located. I often wish I could spend much more time in the wards talking to the patients, but you can see how very busy my days are. These people are so very interesting and friendly and most grateful for all that is being done for them, and love to feel we are interested in them. As the days go on we hear more and more tales of their experiences.

I have some crayon drawings one man did for me. They have been photographed so I shall send you some copies. They were drawn by F. Tannenbaum, a Polish Jew born in Germany, twenty-eight years old and a teacher of languages. He left Germany in 1933, and was arrested by the Gestapo in Madrid, and spent ten years in four concentration camps. He has pulmonary Tb but is walking round and looks after the wireless programmes, assists in the welfare department, and is always coming to my office asking for new clothes. He was liberated by the Americans and then came to Belsen en route to Italy, where he has some friends, but missed the transport and so remained here. In these drawings he depicted various happenings in the concentration camps. He was at Auschwitz No. 174342, Lubin, Maidanek, and Belsen. The drawings are descriptive of his experiences, but tragic. He has all the fingers of his left hand and some on the right hand off at the second joints—the result of frostbite whilst in the camps.

I was invited to be Godmother to an Italian baby, born here on 2nd September. Little Ameri-go Koppa is a fine wee lad and the ceremony went off well. He was called Ameri-go because his mother was liberated by the Americans, before coming to Belsen. The priest from the Vatican Mission officiated and Ameri-go behaved nicely when the water was poured over his head. The ceremony was interesting, the first Roman Catholic one I have attended; the Godfather, who was an Italian DP, held the baby's feet while I held the head. The baby's father died seven months before he was born. The trouble was to find a suitable gift—an American nurse on my staff produced at the eleventh hour a religious medal, which I placed on cotton wool in a match box covered with white paper and enclosed a monetary gift. The mother, resplendent in one of the canary flannelette jackets, sat up in bed and surveyed the ceremony. Both have now gone home and I wonder if I, the child's Godmother, shall ever see him again.

Met a Hungarian doctor today who had done very good work in the Camp both before and since liberation—she was in Auschwitz and told me that the German SS Commander there kept dwarfs and twins as a hobby.

Our hospital is quite interesting at present, we have on an average twenty-five operations per week, from gall bladders to trephines. Some of our patients have been in need of surgical treatment for years. Our surgeon is a German whom I do not like or trust and we always have an anxious time on operation days. He would just arrive at the theatre and say he would operate on so-and-so. We now have an operation list, which must be ready by 4.30 pm the previous day, and the patients are properly prepared. Of course my theatre Sister, Miss Vanderwell, is always present to supervise, and when possible an UNRRA Medical Officer keeps his eye on things and I wander in and out at times.

It has been quite interesting preparing new requisition slips for linen, medical and surgical supplies, hardware, cleaning materials, and stationery, etc. We are terribly short of stock, and before I did this there was a constant and daily stream to each store with all and sundry picking and choosing and, as I said before, no questions asked. I have also worked out an average of soap and cleaning materials required for each ward and issue them once weekly, and have taken over the surgical supply stores from the British sergeant. The 3000 Russians who are patients in the Squares at present had priority in the latter for some unknown reason and had pretty well cleared out the stock before we took control. Now my Canadian assistant is the big chief and holds the key.

Thermometers are practically extinct—only three to one hundred Tb patients at present—I have none left in stock, very few in the other wards, and no further supplies available as far as we can see. The German nurses did not attempt to even record dangerous drugs administered. Now I have had treatment forms printed and hope to control things better.

I commenced to tell you how interesting it all is. We have patients with typhus, typhoid, meningitis, diphtheria, scarlet fever, osteomyelitis, and a number of babies with gastro-enteritis at present, and of course many still with pulmonary Tb and other medical complaints.

I am now setting up a new children's and a sick babies' ward. Had some patchwork quilts and knitted coverlets given me from England and they do brighten up the cots. We are looking for some pictures for the walls and have collected a few odd toys. I am also having bed socks, jackets and mittens made by the DP welfare workers (who were in Camp 1), and my layette sets have lovely cream blankets for the maternity ward. We have thirty-eight beds there and the same number of cots—British Tommy pattern—so expect a busy time! The stork has been busy and they say there are 500 pregnant women in camp at present.

One night we went into Celle, a quaint town on the River Aller, some three-quarters of an hour's drive from here, across Luneberg Heath, and our nearest British Army PO for purchasing stamps and air letters. We hear that Kramer of the Horror Camp and a number of his male and female fellow creatures were imprisoned there until removed recently to Luneberg for the grand trial. The house of Hanover is situated on the side of a lake in Celle and we were invited to a concert by the RAF in the private theatre of the great yellow Schloss, wherein the late 16th Century William

Duke of Luneberg and progenitor of the Royal House of Hanover and Windsor lived. Built like an opera house, the theatre has three tiers of circular galleries in white and gold with crimson curtains, carpets and upholstering, and a lovely crystal chandelier suspended from the ceiling. The performers were Germans and we wondered how Paule Lampe felt when playing our National Anthem. It sounded grand in that German Theatre! One pianist, Gertrud Wehl-Rosenfeld, an icily aloof female whose technique was perfect but whose playing lacked feeling, refused to play one of the items listed as variations in D Major Op 76 by Beethoven and said it was a mistake on the programme. I cannot remember if it is the work with the theme on which the Victory song we heard so often over the air during the war is based—but somehow think that was one of his symphonies—anyway, she refused to play it for some reason and substituted a composition I did not know.

We have just heard that the UNRRA training centre in France has been closed for investigation by CIB 1. There are over 1000 people there and it is rumoured there have been many arrests. In an international organisation such as this, so hurriedly got together, there are bound to be some whose scruples are not up to standard—some personnel who are unsuitable, others incompetent and others who openly state that they do not intend to work. That makes it increasingly difficult for those who are nearly distracted because they can't get on with the job they came to do. However, one would imagine that this could have been avoided because they were careful enough regarding our credentials, goodness only knows! When I think how I sat up till 2 am filling in those minutely detailed forms on which I had to state my life history and all salary received since I commenced earning! They must have been staggered in Washington in these days of soaring salaries to read that I began my teaching career at the age of sixteen on £25 per year, plus fares.

The UNRRA Welfare Officer, a Czech woman, had arrived at last, but unfortunately has been appointed Hospital registrar. Her husband, who had been in the Horror Camp, died after liberation, on the day before she arrived to see him. It was very sad; she has one girl at school in England.

Except for three DP girls working under a French welfare worker from the Vatican Mission, we have had no one to take that burden from our shoulders. The patients lack occupation and we have practically no handcraft supplies, needles, cottons or materials. There is little reading matter available either. A number of Polish books did arrive but when censored were found to be mostly political propaganda, so were banned. The patients are very clever with their fingers and have made some attractive things from scraps and threads drawn from towels, blankets, and other odd bits of material we can find. We all hope some supplies will be forthcoming soon, for at this time when occupation is as important as nursing care, productive occupation could be organised so easily. Half my patients sit all day long with idle hands and are capable and anxious to help. They have made knitting needles from bicycle spokes and knit gauze strips into lovely brushed pullovers. Do you think you could collect me some felt, leather, chamois, coloured silks and thread, raffia, cotton, needles, etc., so that some of these clever fingers will find occupation for the winter? One of the patients recently made the SMO and me lovely baskets of heather gathered in the woods, and another gave me some heather framed like a picture, as a memento. These tokens of appreciation are so spontaneous and mean so much.

There are so many of the ordinary things to be done, which we take for granted in our well-established hospitals. It is intensely interesting, if only we had time and sufficient supervisory staff to assist. There was no regular system of admissions previously and patients admitted and discharged themselves—and still do! We had numbers who returned several times from the Camp to our nice comfortable hospital with wireless, good food, and freedom to sleep in the fields all night or bring their friends home to bed as they desired. We gradually instituted visiting hours, but they still go out. Some acute Tbs still wander in their pyjamas in the wet—they like it—they have been so used to it for so long and this freedom means so much to them.

Talking of our hospital pyjamas—they are the same as the convict garb worn in the Horror Camp and some of the patients hate them. Now I am trying to arrange to have them dyed; even if they turn out navy blue, they'd prefer them to the broad, dark blue and white stripes that remind them of so much. They don't seem to feel the cold, their bodies must have been adjusted in those awful years. They like the blankets, however, just as much as ever, and only today, we have since been told by another patient, a visitor

A gift to Muriel Doherty from one of the patients at Belsen: heather framed like a picture

walked off with one tucked under his arm. The ensemble suits with beret to match in pale grey look very smart and are much more interesting than blankets!

The Chief Nursing Officer, Allied Control Commission, called on me the other day and brought with her Frau Oberin Von Oetzen, Matron in Chief, German Red Cross Nursing Sisterhood, and Frau Oberin Vollman, her assistant. Both quite charming women to meet, but I could not help thinking all the time how steeped in Nazi cult the Red Cross was. The ACC is endeavouring to find those nurses who were not tainted and it is hard to believe the Matron in Chief could have held her position without being initiated. The Chief Nursing Officer's job is to assist them with the de-Nazification and reconstruction of their nursing services—what a job!

There's something going on behind the scenes at present and we won't be surprised if we suddenly find that we are turned into a training school for German nurses. We are rather concerned—even if we did agree to undertake it, it would be a thankless job; it is difficult enough now to improve their bedside nursing, which is becoming worse and is probably a manifestation of passive resistance. I don't think I could train German nurses—I didn't volunteer for that. Even though it might be said it would improve the treatment received by the patients, I don't agree, because we are too few to supervise it.

We have another SS man in hospital, a nasty piece of work, under double guard day and night. He has about six known murders to his credit, I believe, and has endeavoured to convince the UNRRA nurses that he is such an innocent cherub that he would like to join our unit when he is demobilised. We have doubled our vigilance! I believe they all have the SS emblem tattooed in the axilla—but I've not seen it. One of the patients, knowing this, was responsible for the arrest of an SS man who had been admitted under another guise not very long ago.

I have been here two months now and it seems years—none of us knows how long we shall remain, but we hear the Poles will be with us for the winter, or at any rate those who cannot, or will not, return to Poland.

I went to Hamburg last Tuesday. The RAF did their work well. Tense atmosphere, hostile glances from the pasty-faced, apathetic, skinny German inhabitants. Nothing in the shops worth buying, but it was interesting. We had tea at the British Officers' Club in a large hotel and crossed the River Elbe several times in our journeyings. Whole areas of the city are in ruins and no cleaning up done yet. They say Berlin is even worse.

Today I have 112 trained German nurses and nineteen German Nurse Helps—nine of the trained nurses are Red Cross Wehrmacht nurses. All the uniforms are very untidy. I believe when the German nurses were first brought in, the DPs purloined a large number of their clothes, and the British Army Matron scoured the country for replacements, hence the motley collection.

Aprons of all varieties, ancient and modern; caps not so bad, as the pattern of the majority is similar and really quite smart. However, the hair is worn at all lengths and angles, which does not enhance their appearance, and some caps are worn like onion bags to enclose the hair hanging down the back. I have now arranged for uniforms to be laundered (they have been washing their own) and hope for better things. Then there was the question of soap—that priceless commodity. There was no issue for the German nurses and so the wards never had enough! Now we have given authority for the Germans to purchase locally (they get the equivalent of about £2 per month salary). Shoes were another problem—all soles seem to be wooden in Germany now and some of the nurses' shoes were dreadful. How they walked in them I do not know. We got a supply for them for which they paid.

When we first came here we were told that the UNRRA Medical Director had said that the success of UNRRA in the British Zone depended on the success we made of Belsen. Every one of my staff has risen to this challenge, but we have received little co-operation from UNRRA local HQ to date. The UNRRA nursing staff is quite inadequate for the work we have to do and is to be reduced to twelve, I believe, including myself. I have never had more than sixteen and this only for a day or two.

From the 8000–10 000 patients who were at Belsen when I arrived, we are now reduced to 500. Evacuations have taken place, sometimes at the rate of 350 a day or more, to Czechoslovakia, Yugoslavia and Sweden. The last of the children went to Sweden at the end of July and a number have died, so that their hospital is closed. The Round House is also closed, as you know, and the Squares are still invaded by some 3000 of the Red Army—nearly all men from the Ruhr with Tb. These are nursed by German nurses but we have nothing to do with them.

UNRRA is responsible for the Glyn Hughes Hospital and its annexes. The patients now are nearly all Poles and Jews, with a few Italians, Czechs, Lithuanians and Yugoslavs. Many will never leave. When I took over, my job was to reorganise an emergency hospital into a normal institution—and what a heartbreaking undertaking with a handful of UNRRA nurses! Eight of my staff at present are Public Health nurses with no experience in and little desire for hospital nursing. They were very surprised and disappointed when they found they were assigned to Belsen Hospital and not to field jobs. However, they have been a marvellous help whilst awaiting re-assignment, but it does not make things easy to have constant change, especially when so many of the staff are inexperienced in hospital administration and used to a nine-to-five day.

Later: 18th September 1945

We were invited by the Central Jewish Committee, Culture Department to its first concert the other evening. It was held in connection with their New Year Festivities on 15th September, for which we are endeavouring to collect sufficient candles for each patient to have one on his locker.

Although tragic, it was very well done. Most of the scenes and plays depicted episodes from their Concentration Camp Life and their persecution. *The Goel* (Messiah), by Emile Bernhart, was depicted by a Jew hiding in a cellar, and *The Mother's Dance*, by Doli Kotz, showed a mother in a Concentration Camp after the death of her baby. *The Tailors*, by Lulbak, with eight performers, told a tale of past and future, and the entire company produced the Kazet Theatre—showing how the inmates of a Concentration Camp kept their spirits up with music after the SS guards had left them without food or light.

We knew it was all so real—and what suffering!

There certainly is a great national awakening to their own rights and one wonders where it will lead them—I feel many who have not known these people under these conditions may never understand.

I am looking forward to the food parcels which I hear are arriving shortly in large numbers from my friends in Australia. We have sufficient food ourselves from our Army rations; margarine and occasionally butter, no eggs or egg powder, nor fresh milk, but plenty of potatoes and occasional fresh vegetables and always vitamin tablets. Some Australian luxuries for the sick patients will be lovely, but we ourselves are very well fed. I tried to get a special issue of butter for the UNRRA nurses on the grounds that they were nursing Tb patients but was unsuccessful.

Life is exceedingly interesting and exceedingly busy at present—never a dull moment. Weddings, christenings, dances, concerts, sports and open-air entertainment—always something going on in and around the Hospital.

My German progresses slowly, my French conversation with Mademoiselle Jorlan, Welfare Officer of the Vatican Mission, is grand as long as I remain silent, and you can imagine how voluble my chats with my Italian godson were. Our housekeeper, who arrived so late, has done practically nothing since she came and is leaving tomorrow, complete with dog! It is apparently taken for granted that I shall be in charge of the Mess, but I have been firm in asserting that the Matron is not responsible for a mixed mess (in more ways than one) and certainly I'm much too busy to be conducting a residential restaurant for every odd UNRRA transient driver or member on leave who comes along to have a look at Belsen, as they frequently do!

The electricity and water still go off two or three times a day, and the light is failing now so will finish this.

Later

The trial of the SS man from Belsen opened in Luneberg on 17th September. The one we had under double guard in hospital with post-typhus complications has been transferred there. He is a perfect specimen of brutality.

The curfew tolls at 10.30 pm now and the guards have orders to shoot to kill. We have a special pass if out after that time, but we don't take any risks. We nearly always have someone in Hospital under guard these days. This is a copy of one of the latest notice posted:

MILITARY GOVERNMENT—GERMANY—BRITISH ZONE

Attention All Displaced Persons

LAW AND ORDER WILL BE MAINTAINED

1. British troops have been ordered to SHOOT TO KILL any person no matter what nationality, who is found committing any crime, or tries to evade arrest.
2. More extensive measures of control are being taken during the hours of darkness.
3. All persons must assist in combating lawlessness. Information which will lead to the arrest of culprits must be given to the proper authorities.
4. CRIME means any act against the peace, the property, and well being of any person or the community as a whole.

5 The curfew which extends from 22.30 hours to 04.30 hours until April 1946 applies to all persons irrespective of nationality. No one must be out of doors during these times unless in possession of a Military Government Exemption Certificate.

YOU ARE WARNED!

Chapter 7

THE WHOLE SEAL OF NAZI CRUELTY

F. Tannenbaum, 'Life in Concentration Camp' series, Belsen, 1945

Belsen
16th September 1945

Among the residents of Belsen are some survivors of a party of 800 young girls who were marched on foot from Bremen to Belsen shortly before the camp entered upon its final phase of horror. They had been used as street-sweepers in Bremen, many were barefooted and scantily clad. They were three days on the march without food. Their guards carried lashes, and when the girls sang on the way they were cruelly kicked and thrashed.

In September 1944 another group of 500 girls, Czech slave workers, were transported from Auschwitz extermination camp in Poland to the most dangerous industrial area in Hamburg. When the British bombing increased in ferocity over that city, they were all hurriedly evacuated to Belsen under terrible conditions.

The following story, told to a British Red Cross representative by a young Czech Jewess—I shall call her Lenka—speaks for itself. On 22nd January, 1942 she and her parents were arrested and sent by the Germans to a transit camp in Pilsen, where they remained for three days, their only crime being that they were Jews. They were only allowed 50 kg of luggage—all their worldly possessions. There were 2600 persons in this camp and all were given an identification number. After three days they were taken to the station, guarded all the time by German police with rifles which they did not hesitate to use. The temperature was 30°C below zero, with snow and ice. The train was not heated and when the doors were opened they almost froze. The journey to Theresienstadt, Czechoslovakia, normally took three hours, but this train took fifteen. There was no station in the village, so they were forced to walk in snow and ice for one hour carrying their baggage.

During the journey they were told that a dreadful event had happened in the camp a few days before. Eleven young men were publicly hanged for writing a letter to their parents saying they were hungry. A little later nine boys were hanged for the same reason. One lad sang a national revolutionary song whilst standing below the gallows. To have an alibi before the world, the Nazis ordered a Jew to hang his own nationals—but no Jew would undertake this.

Finally, the Germans found a man, Adolf Fischer, whose civilian trade was an employee in the Institute of Anatomy at Prague University Medical School, to carry out the awful deed.

The Czechs carried no beds or bedding, only a little straw. All the men were separated out two days after arriving at their destination. Children said goodbye to fathers, wives to husbands. The barracks were locked and guarded by the SS police. No one was allowed to leave or enter without permission from the SS Commander, and only a very few were so privileged.

At first they were only required to work voluntarily. Lenka worked in the office of the food ration cards. Men tried to work in the potato cellar because they sometimes had the opportunity of seeing their womenfolk when pushing a cart of potatoes. There were no horses or lorries to move these heavy loads—only human beings.

Punishment for a woman who was caught talking to a man was banishment to a concentration camp in Poland. Every two or three months, many thousands were moved from Theresienstadt to make way for new transports. Old people of sixty-five years and over were among those moved. Most of them died on the journey, those who survived went to the gas chambers.

On 10th April 1942, Lenka continues, 1000 women up to forty years of age were sent to Kavohlat, a country place in the Bohemian Forest. They were to remain and plant trees. 'I was among these women in a small group of forty-five girls. When the train left Theresienstadt we thought we were to be free, but were very soon disappointed.'

Guarded by four armed police, they had to walk for four hours to their lodgings—an old inn without light and with locked windows. The doors were guarded day and night by the police. They rose at 6 am and were given one litre of watery soup for breakfast. At 7 am the game-keeper came to fetch them. It was a fifty-minute walk to the wood. Each one was issued with a basket of young trees and a pickaxe with which to plant the forest. Ten girls were in Lenka's party, with an old workman as guard who would not allow them to move farther away than ten metres because he had been told they were dangerous prisoners who would escape! The first day was so horrible that they were crying nearly all day. It was windy, very cold and raining. At 7 pm they were marched home for supper. The food issue was 2 kg of bread for eight days, one litre of watery soup, and a very small supper after a twelve-hour working day.

Writing letters was forbidden but Lenka and a friend managed to send letters to their relatives at home, who tried to visit the girls but found it was too dangerous.

After two months of this awful life, the party returned to Theresienstadt, which had become a ghetto, and a process of deliberate extermination commenced. The inmates had to make German uniforms, boxes for munitions and artistic things. All Christians were removed from the camp, and new Jewish transports arrived. Most of these unfortunate prisoners were old German Jews. They were forced to lie on the squalid floor, starving and infested with lice. They died of hunger, 'a picture of misery' as Lenka described them. In contrast to this awfulness, a large coffee house was built in the camp. A jazz band provided music for supposed concerts and a theatre. Girls were dressed in black with white aprons and acted as waitresses. The smartest girl prisoners were obliged to swim in the modern swimming pool, and life in the ghetto was filmed. German propaganda for the public!

In December 1943 the SS Commander ordered about eighty persons to Poland as there were too many young people in the ghetto. Lenka was working in the central office at this time and was one of those selected. Her parents accompanied her voluntarily.

The transit camp to which they were sent was a long way from the station. A big open fire was used to light the SS Commandant's table. The prisoners were filed past and were hurriedly packed into a truck with their luggage. There were fifty-five persons and Adolf Fischer, the hangman of Theresienstadt, whom Lenka described as 'an awful companion for travelling'. The journey lasted thirty dreadful hours, which were spent in vainly trying to obtain some seating space for her parents and herself.

On arrival at Auschwitz extermination camp in Poland at 10 pm they found the SS and men in striped clothing armed with sticks, waiting for them. They soon learned that these men were prisoners who were forced to work for the SS. The victims were bundled out of the truck very quickly and were told to leave their baggage behind as they could collect it the next day, but they never saw it again. The remainder of the night was spent sitting on the bare floor of a hut. Early next morning the men were separated from the women and all were driven out to wait in the snow, not knowing what was to happen to them. After some interminable hours they were told they were going to the bath, which was a long distance away. The thought of a bath was very welcome, as such luxuries were unknown in the camps.

When they set out, all old people who could not walk were left in the snow to freeze. On the way they passed large numbers of people who had died during the journey and had been thrown out of the lorries. Others not yet dead were put amongst them. They finally arrived, exhausted, at a hut, where they were obliged to remain two days and nights guarded by an SS woman with a big dog, who used her gun whenever she disliked anything.

They were given no food or drink. Lenka says, 'I think I never had such a thirst than at this time. We gave our watches and precious things we wore for a cup of water. We were not allowed to leave the hut, even for the lavatory. Most people became deranged. It was horrible, they were shouting and crying the whole night.'

Suddenly they were ordered out of the blocks, not knowing what was to happen. They were taken to another hut where a Polish girl prisoner branded them on the left forearm with a number. Lenka says, 'Even little children got it and they cried so much because it ached.'

This was the tattooing of the official concentration camp number, which so many of our patients wear today. I have been told that when the numbers ran into hundreds of thousands at Auschwitz, the SS prefixed a letter for record purposes, thus hiding the actual number of their victims (which amounted to several millions in this camp alone) from the world.

After some hours of waiting they arrived at the bath huts. An SS woman took all watches, wedding rings and other jewellery. They were forced to undress and leave their clothing behind. This they never saw again. They were marched under a shower, but were not dried and had to wait many hours for the prison clothes, which consisted of thin summer dresses and coats, on which were their numbers. You will remember it was the middle of a severe winter. They were then marched to the political office and had to sign a document which they were not allowed to read. Lenka saw that the heading was 'Concentration Camp Auschwitz' so for the first time they knew where they were. Even before the end of the war this camp was already known as the worst camp in Europe, and one from which no one ever escaped.

They were kept waiting for hours, surrounded with dead bodies, they were sitting among them. Girl prisoners who had been in the camp a long time and whose morale was broken whipped and beat them with leather belts. Do not condemn any man or woman for this—because prisoners in the camps earned extra rations if they worked thus for the Nazis, and a starving human will do anything in order to obtain food. Late that night they were driven to the family camp, closely guarded by SS men and dogs. In the block in which they were to sleep were three-tiered bunks, one above the other, two metres long, eight centimetres wide. Five girls and later seven and eight slept in three such bunks. Their food was a hunk of dry bread and half a litre of water per day.

Two days later the men arrived, and on Christmas Day, for some extraordinary and probably sadistic reason, the SS allowed them to meet their womenfolk for a few minutes. They were almost unrecognisable, but happy to meet again after those terrible days of horror. During the first few days they were not required to work at all, but the SS came and forced them from their bunks. You can imagine how weak they were. Later they were forced to carry heavy stones from early morning to 3 pm. Lenka says, 'It was hard work walking with heavy stones.'

On arrival home they had to stay *appell*, which means they attended a roll call at which the SS men counted them. These *appells* sometimes lasted three to four hours, during which they were standing outside the block half frozen. After the *appell* the wire which surrounded the camp was charged with electricity, which meant instantaneous death for anyone touching it.

Four weeks after their arrival at Auschwitz, war work production was commenced. All young girls were forced to work from 6 am to 5 pm. Belts for rifles were made of 'such a queer sort of stuff, that our skin was quite black, which did not come off on washing'. The death rate was high—bodies were piled on trucks covered with dirty sacks and pushed by the men prisoners to the crematorium. Lenka says, 'I lost my father in this camp and I can never visit his grave because he has none—it was dreadful for me. I was not allowed to visit him for five days and when I did, I found he had died in the meantime.'

On 7th March the order came that all those who had arrived in the transport three and a half months before were to be moved to another concentration camp. Lenka said they were congregated in the transit blocks and during the night orders from the SS men were heard, followed by shouting and the noise of weeping, unhappy people being forced into lorries. Three thousand, five hundred young, healthy people were sent to the gas chamber that night. Those who remained in the family camp were told they would be quarantined there for six months. Their registration cards were marked *sender behandling* (special treatment), which they knew meant gas. The next three months were terrible—they suffered so much and counted the weeks and days to their death. This was the Nazi method of adding to their agonies. 'It is a fearful feeling if you know the date you have to die.'

The day came and nothing happened—some days later a great *selection* was announced. Men and women between the age of sixteen and forty had to pass, quite naked, before the SS doctor and guards. Sometimes a band, selected from the prisoners, was playing. Always the savage dogs, leather whips and guns were there, and used without mercy. Those who were considered useful to the Nazis in any way at all were marched one way, those not required the other. It all depended on the good humour of the doctor and the guards whether the prisoner went to slave work or the gas chamber.

On 1st July 1944, 1000 men left the family camp. The following day 1000 women were sent to the great women's section of Auschwitz. They were stripped of all they had and forced to stand naked outside before they bathed. An old dirty dress (no underwear, shoes or stockings) was given to each. Sixteen girls were living and sleeping in a few bunks one and a half metres square. Lenka was amongst them. Food was dreadful. 'Nine girls or more had to eat watery soup from the same bowl, without a spoon. I could not even look at it.' From 3 am they had to remain on the *appell* to 8 or 9 am without shoes or stockings. They were not allowed to wash or go to the lavatory. They were beaten if they disobeyed. 'This hell lasted three days which seemed endless.' Then followed another selection. 'My mother and I came through.' Imagine the mental torment of it all!

That evening they were sent to the bath and everyone was given a grey frock and underwear. Next morning their hair was cut and everyone got a piece of bread. 'And then the miracle happened. We were marched to the station—the first worker transport in the history of Auschwitz, the first people with numbers on their arms, to leave Auschwitz; nobody before had ever left this horror camp.'

They travelled in cattle trucks, one hundred girls in one truck, guarded by German soldiers. For two days they travelled, not knowing where they were going. Suddenly, the train stopped in Hamburg where SS guards were waiting. 'Our homes were big corn stores in the harbour of Hamburg, which was built on the Elbe.'

They had to work in big oil factories where they cleaned and rebuilt smashed parts. 'It was a bad life, we had nothing at all, no towels, no tooth-brush, no soap, nothing, nothing, only our naked life. We had to get up at 3.30 am in the morning; at 5 am we went to the ship and then we had to walk half an hour to the factory, where we were working to 6 o'clock at night.'

They arrived back at the corn stores at 8 pm and had dinner—one litre of watery soup, a fifth of a loaf of bread—sometimes quarter of a skin of sausage. This was the only food they had all day. At 10 pm they went to bed. 'One hour later the English came and bombarded Hamburg.' The corn stores were in one of the most dangerous parts of the city. The girls had to remain on the second floor, the guard locked the door and 'ran to the bunker (air raid shelter). He promised to return if there were some danger, but he never did.' The building trembled, they saw bombs fall and pieces of the walls fell on their heads. This happened every night, so that they had no more than three and a half hours' sleep. They were tired to death.

During the daytime, when working in the factories, they were allowed to go to the bunker only at *Vollalarm* and then they had to run half an hour through artificial fog. They were guarded all the time by German soldiers and were not allowed to take ten steps without asking a guard. Nearby, some French prisoners of war were working and they tried to help the women, but they were strictly forbidden to speak to them. At great risk they exchanged letters with political views and gave them hope that the war would end soon.

In September 1944, 500 Czech girls, including Lenka, were

moved to a small workers camp near Hamburg. An area in the woods surrounded by barbed wire, containing two blocks, was their home. Life was, if possible, still harder than in Hamburg. 'Less to eat and harder work . . . Smashed buildings and channels for water supply, sand and bricks; hunger and the beginning of winter was our life . . . on our feet were worn wooden shoes; old torn rags in place of stockings. The coats we got in winter were marked by yellow crosses, holes had to be cut in the back, the sleeves were exchanged from other coats, that was the way of our dressing to be recognised by everybody immediately as a prisoner . . . no heating on return from work . . . a two-hour walk, only cold rooms, and often the news that the kitchen would not prepare food, having no coal or wood. So we went weeping and frozen, hungry and desolated to our cold beds.'

The girls were obliged to go after work to the forest to cut trees, which they had to carry home through the forest covered in ice and snow. Their clothes and shoes were saturated and never dried as they had to wear them the next day.

'Day and night,' she says, 'the Tommies sent the bombs over our heads. We could not go to the bunker and had to spend the terrible hours during worktime on the workplace, looking up to the sky and counting the planes . . . Nearly the whole time we were without water and electricity as the works were bombarded every day.'

They were moved to a camp at Tiefstock in the most dangerous part of Hamburg.

> A camp not yet ready, wet, cold, and without any furniture, was our home . . . It stood in the middle of a large factory court . . . on the right was the Hamburg electricity works, on the left the gas works, railways, important bridges and industries. The camp was bombarded every day and night and completely devastated. Many women were killed and wounded, but some escaped . . . interesting was the scene before the gate of the camp, this day. My group was just returning from the factory (we made cement bricks by hand) when the bombardment began and the planes were already flying over our heads. We hurried to come in and to hide ourselves in the primitive earthy hole called bunker. Because we were not yet counted (thirty girls) by the SS Commander, the gate guard did not allow us to

enter the camp. Therefore, the greatest part of the girls did not reach the bunker in time and found the death.

They were now without shelter, but it was March and the sun began to shine. They lived in the ruins of the camp. The Germans did not supply workers to repair the buildings, so they were obliged to rebuild the camp after coming home from work.

The British were expected in Hamburg, so the SS Commander was ordered to send away the secret files. Lenka knew this as her mother worked as his secretary. All documents were packed in a great hurry and they left the next morning. After travelling three days and two nights (the lines were blocked so that they were held up for many hours at a station or returned to Hamburg), under terrible circumstances, they reached Bergen-Belsen.

Lenka describes this journey as:

> . . . fearful. Crazy SS women accompanied us, throwing stones into the crowd of women, who were one hundred in one truck. We had no place to sit or to lie, we could not leave the truck for the lavatory. It was a desolate situation, people got mad and some died in this fearful way, from hunger, thirst and desolation . . . Arriving at Bergen-Belsen we were surprised by another fearful aspect . . . Hundreds of trucks with dead and dying men were standing in the railway station. Their bodies were blue and bloody skeletons, the faces wounded, the dirty clothing torn and full of lice. That was the so-called transport of men to Bergen-Belsen . . . This transport never reached its place of destination . . . We, on our way from the station to the camp, had to reflect about the purpose of our coming here. The result was very bad . . . We saw lots of old, torn, dirty clothes and shoes, no people at all and a hidden camp in the forest. We did not think anything else than that we came to an empty camp, where transports are killed by some unknown way . . . The more we were witnesses of so many German crimes, we knew that these beasts did not wish us to over-live the war . . . The liberation was so near, we were full of hope and had to die just now, after having spent the hard years of prison, after having felt the whole seal of German cruelty . . . God did not hear our prayers . . . He led us through all the dangers to forget us in the moment where liberation is coming. These were the ideas of a desolated crowd of hungry and tired women . . . And the miracle happened again . . . we did not die . . . The 15th April 1945 was the miraculous day when the

> second British Army liberated Bergen-Belsen . . . We greeted our saviours with deepest thankfulness and never will forget this historical day, which gave us back our lives.

I have been wanting to send you this story for some time now but had to wait until I was able to have a day off—which I have been enjoying today. It is so typical of the sufferings of these young slave workers that it will help you to understand their reactions.

To: Miss Udell, Chief Nursing Adviser, UNRRA
Date: 24th September 1945
Subject: Report on Nursing Matters

UNRRA Matron and Nursing Staff took over Glyn Hughes Hospital on 13th August 1945. At time of transfer the general impression gained was that there was a lack of organisation of work and duties, with much time worked and poor supervision and deceptive levels of nursing and domestic staff!

The wards were untidy, masses of clothing cluttered the beds, dusty china accumulating on lockers at mid-morning, afternoon and evening. Curtains draped many windows in wards where patients with advanced pulmonary tuberculosis were nursed. There was gross but unavoidable overcrowding and little classification or segregation of patients. Advanced cases of pulmonary Tb were nursed side by side with non-Tb cases. Old tins, jam dishes and jars (the majority of which were without lids) were used as sputum mugs and no apparent disinfectant or sterilisation was carried out. Large numbers of flies were seen in the wards and kitchen, swarming over the uncovered food and the helpless patients. There were no bed nets available. As there were no visiting hours, there was a constant stream of people in and out of the hospital wards day and night. There were some twenty-six holes in the fence, so that the guards on duty at the hospital gate were unable to control entry.

The Matron of the British General Hospital stated that severe losses of soap, food rations, linen and blankets were occurring, in fact she had uncovered a very large collection of fresh eggs, butter, tinned food and comforts hidden in the linen cupboard between the folds of sheets, etc. The key to this cupboard was carried by the Oberschwester! . . . On taking over the hospital on 13th August 1945 it was found that the bedside care was of a poor standard in spite of the fact that the majority of German nurses were trained.

Nursing care was mechanical and unfinished—the technique poor. The sick male patients were not being sponged and little attempt was made to encourage patients to eat, large unappetising helpings often being left at the bedside. There was little initiative or imagination as to the patients' mental comfort and as they are easily upset over small matters of food and clothing, this often led to disturbances which, with a little tact, could have been avoided.

There were numerous instances of treatment being ordered by the Medical Officer but not carried out, or carried out many hours after the specified time. No record was made of the ordering of dangerous drugs and dosages appeared often to be left to the German nurses to decide. Operations were performed by the German doctors at any time without previous warning to the theatre staff. There were no reports of patients kept in the wards. The supply of thermometers was small and totally inadequate for the number and type of patients in the hospital, etc.

Hohne (Belsen) Assembly Centre
27th September 1945

How the time flies—I never seem to have time to do all I want to. My writing efforts are curtailed by the fact that the supply of coal is very short indeed, and therefore electricity has to be restricted. As we depend on the latter for the pumping of our water supply, we are still without water or electricity at certain hours during the day and night. Candles are almost unprocurable and we only have a few flat German night-light types left. Although we have ninety lanterns, only ten can be used because the other eighty do not burn kerosene, and the special fuel is unprocurable.

I found a baby hurricane lantern in the *Keller* the other day, which I reserved for my own very restricted use and wonder each time how much longer the oil will last. Unfortunately, the hours they choose to economise with light include 7–8 pm or later, and as the days are drawing in we cannot depend on twilight.

Yesterday, without any warning, we found ourselves without water or electricity from 7.30 am to 8.30 pm, with no opportunity to fill available receptacles—imagine a 500-bed hospital caught like that! We were irate when the electricity came on at 8.30 pm as that was the time of a special cabaret at the officers' club, for which the organisers had procured many coloured lights, etc. They told us that the transformer at Brunswick was at fault, but coincidences are strange and it would have been a pity to waste those lights! Anyway, being prepared with some precious candles in gin bottles at dinner tonight, we were amazed to find the light only off for half an hour. Great plans were therefore made for hot baths. I have mentioned already the large cumbersome bath heaters, which are really meant for the steam-radiator system, but which can be heated with wood, of which there is no shortage here. We had a lovely blaze going half an hour ago and, suddenly, off went the light and water. I am now waiting for the heater to blow up!

Enough of our ablution problems. We had a dance in the hospital today, complete with orchestra, in one of our spacious corridors which fan out leading to two other off-spring wards. The old piano squawked bravely above the drums and the pulmonary

Tbs danced with anyone who came along. Everyone loved it. Girls with legs in plaster discarded crutches and pirouetted around, young men in the dreadful striped concentration camp pyjamas (which I have been unable to have dyed) swirled round with Gypsy women in colourful long, full skirts, and the visitors joined in. I even saw one or two of the German cleaning women taking part surreptitiously. The noise was awful and everyone enjoyed themselves immensely.

Hospital Administrators, wake up—your wards are much too dull. Why not let the medical and surgical cases mix more? Shirt tails and pyjamas would be much more becoming on the dance floor than evening frocks and swallow tails, and a hospital patients' orchestra would certainly liven things up and lengthen their stay in hospital!

Interval here when the light unexpectedly flashed on—I dashed to retrieve what was left of the fire in the bath heater, which didn't burst, and when it was just nicely blazing, out popped the light again.

Talking of baths, the other day Piri complained of not feeling well. She had been forced to give a pint of blood per month in the Concentration Camp and I think she is probably anaemic. I arranged with one of our doctors for her to be examined at 1 pm and to make quite sure, rang the mess to ask Mili, our Czech cook supervisor, to tell Frau Rosa Kramer (our housekeeper in charge of DPs working in the Nurses' mess) to see that Piri was ready for the doctor. She said she understood me quite well. At 1 pm Doctor entered the portals to find that Frau Kramer, after bowing her in, took her by the arm and led her to the bathroom, proudly announcing a lovely steaming bath. Bewildered, she explained it was Piri she wanted, not a bath. However, undaunted, the Frau, having produced Piri, indulged in the bath herself. These language problems! Why ever was there a Tower of Babel?

Quite a stir in hospital last week. About 5 pm a convoy of trucks, armoured cars and other vehicles, all bristling with arms, high-ranking officers, and red caps (the British service police) with their guns at the ready, without warning, drove round our circular drive and out again. Word flew round that it was Kramer and his beastly men and women, but we now hear it was some of the prosecution and the witnesses who had been brought to visit the

Horror Camp and who probably were being shown the modern Glyn Hughes Hospital so near, and in such contrast.

I am going to the trial in Luneberg on Monday. It opened two weeks ago, and should be very interesting; shall tell you all about it in a later letter.

I've decided a great deal of unnecessary expense is incurred, and time lost, in our Australian hospitals by admitting women and keeping them in hospital for certain operations! A Russian doctor from the camp borrowed our theatre one morning this week and brought with him the patient whom, I assume, was a Russian camp follower. No anaesthetic, nor pre-medication nor preparation of any kind. She walked out of the theatre afterwards and left for Russia the next day. Unfortunately, follow-up notes will not be possible!

On Tuesday last, 25th September, I was invited to Camp 1 to the unveiling of a Jewish memorial to the thousands of Jews who are buried there and the hundreds of thousands more who perished elsewhere. I think it was the Day of Atonement. Thousands of Jewish survivors (and there are about 9000 at present in this camp) and other DPs marched from the present camp carrying banners of blue and white with various mottoes. The granite memorial is erected near one of the immense graves holding thousands of nameless people who were either dead or died soon after liberation, before the British were able to evacuate them. We drove there and, standing on an elevated piece of ground, were able to watch the seemingly endless procession as it approached. So many had been in the Horror Camp, and many had lost all their people there, while others had come to pay tribute to their unfortunate fellows who knew no earthly liberation. While we were waiting for the ceremony to commence, I was introduced to Brigadier Glyn Hughes, who did such famous work at Belsen. I asked him to point out the perimeter of the actual area in which the victims of Nazi brutality had been confined: $\frac{4}{5} \times \frac{2}{5}$ of a mile only, in which more than 50 000 living and unburied dead had been concentrated.

The ceremony was in Yiddish and the Rabbi, who spoke from one of the German observation posts, was evidently very melodramatic for he moved the multitude so that the sobbing came as the soft twittering of many birds in distant trees at dusk. It was terrible. I stood on the bonnet of our car and was able to look down on the crowd, mostly young men and women. You could pick out

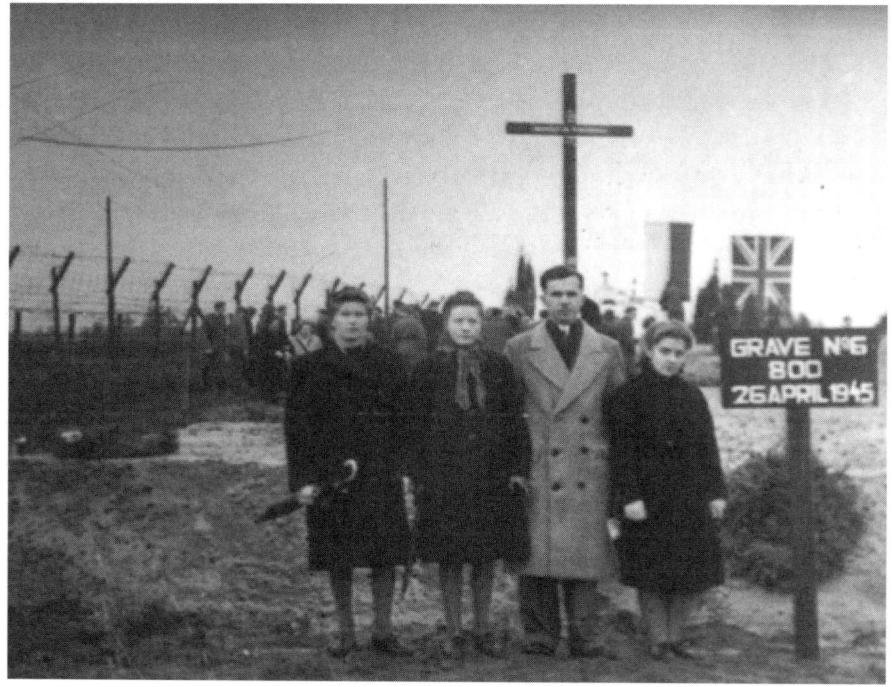

Displaced persons at Mass Grave No. 6, Belsen, 1945

many of those who had been in the Horror Camp—their hair had grown fine and sparse, due to illness and starvation. One officer, pointing out the observation posts, told me that when the prisoners broke through just before liberation and many of the SS guards had either been killed or fled, the Hungarian soldiers had target practice from these fourteen or fifteen elevated posts surrounding the area. They are the creatures who now strut about here and do as little work as they can. We hear they may be returning to Hungary soon and no one will miss them, I am sure.

The other day, Wille Lubbe, a German Jewish DP and one of the interpreters at the Hospital, burst into my office waving a bundle of papers—all his credentials, identity cards, personal papers, which he had hidden in France two and a half years ago from the Gestapo. He was overjoyed and almost hugged me. 'Worth more than millions of francs to me,' he cried. He fought in the International Communist Brigade in the Spanish War also and now is entering Hospital with Tb. 'I am now a man of honour,' he explained, 'and

I could return to France where I had worked in the Underground Movement, but I prefer to stay until the last SS man is killed.'

This is the story of his experiences as he wrote it:

> I have been six years in three different concentration camps. When the civil war in Spain was lost, we were obliged to find shelter and protection in France. It was in February 1939, the French Government at this time sent us all into concentration camps. We were badly treated. During our years we were slave workers. Then came the German invasion of Holland, Belgium and France. The French Authorities delivered me to the German Gestapo. After six months in jail without a trial I was sent to the concentration camp in Sachsenhausen, because I was anti-Nazi and fought in Spain against Germany.
>
> During the last two years I have seen terrible things. It is unbelievable that human beings can be so cruel and horrible as the German SS and Gestapo—only to have cut a small piece of leather, a Pole was given fifty strokes, beaten and hanged. We were obliged to see it, not daring to look right or left—this we always had to do when anyone was hanged. There were people every day being shot, and made to suffer all imaginable tortures before death. I saw many young people from all over Europe marked with black crosses on their faces, locked together with hand-cuffs and iron chains on their legs, then they were taken into a barrack room without beds or blankets, and for food they were given a small piece of bread, water once a day, and every third day a small bowl of poor soup. They had to exercise the whole day by rolling on the ground, kneeling up and down until exhausted, and then were shot. We heard them cry by day and night.
>
> I was treated a little better because there was so much work and we were cheap slaves, who could be taken anywhere—white gold, as the SS said. In the morning, before going to work, we were given half a pint of soup or black coffee, twice daily *bettersaves* (some kind of potato cake) often without potatoes; green stuff we never saw. Before going to work we marched from our barracks to the Square in perfect order, then we were counted. The same in the evening when we were marched back to our barracks, very tired, after twelve hours' hard work. On Sunday, we worked till midday but if some of our barracks had not marched in perfect order, or for any other thing—and there was always something wrong—we had to exercise and sing to make believe we were happy.

It is impossible to explain everything the SS found out to make us suffer. We could write home—though there were many who were not allowed—and we were only allowed to say, I am all right, send parcels and money. Our families sent parcels and money, but most of it disappeared. Nazi newspapers were allowed us to read, these we had to pay for ourselves in some way and by them we knew the whole world was working for our liberty. We got news from somewhere of what was going on, that the Allies and Russians were coming. The SS tried to find out where we got the news from, but it was in vain. They took some of our comrades who were known as politicians and the SS tortured and shot them.

In February this year all sick people and I were sent to the camp at Belsen, were told we were going to a lovely sanatorium. I never believed it; when we arrived we all knew we were sent to Belsen Camp to die. By this time, it was being called by the inmates The Camp of Death. First we had to stand for three hours in the rain and cold; the SS tried to count us, but it was impossible because we were all sick and weak. Hundreds lay on the wet ground completely exhausted from the march to the camp from the station, and there were hundreds more dying. All the time we were well guarded by SS shouting and pushing us with guns. The camp was overcrowded with people—no more barracks empty—it rained through the roof, windows were broken, no beds or straw, so we had to spend the night and following days changing with those who slept on the foul and wet ground, and when the barracks were completely full, the rest had to stay outside. Sleep was impossible, because of those who cried in their misery with hunger and pains. Every day in the morning, there were hundreds of deaths, those we had to carry out of the barracks into the square. One day we had 2000; it was because we got every day other columns of sick and dying from other camps. And often lorries full of dead bodies. I worked in the hospital and we noted the deaths daily and must give it to the SS every morning.

In the last six weeks before the English liberated the camp we had 35 000 deaths from ill treatment, typhus and starvation. The total amount of deaths in the camp since I came is more than double that number. During the night, people were obliged to sleep with those who died; there was nothing to be done, you simply pushed the dead bodies on one side, so that one could occupy his place and have a little more room. People became like animals, they took away the food and bread of those who were sick and helpless. The most awful thing was, we found in the mornings bodies cut open and the liver taken out to eat; this was done without it being cooked. It was impossible to find out whether the person was dead or alive when this was done. Another day I saw thirty bodies without ears (cut off) and several where the muscles of the buttocks and backs of the legs had been cut away for food. In April, I fell sick with typhus and then our liberators came. Every one who could rise from his miserable bed went to see and to cheer them, and those who could not go wept, kissing and shouting for joy. I can't express our feelings of thankfulness, knowing that suffering is no more. No more ill treatment; to be again a human being with kindness and help everywhere.

Now the greatest and most noble work for our English liberators came. We were all evacuated into hospital, first the women and children and then the men. We have now clean beds, good food and are treated with so much kindness by our English sisters and orderlies. To the Sister of my ward I wish to express here my most heartfelt thankfulness and deepest feelings to her. She was our Mother, never tired to help us and glad to see us happy. I will never forget Sister and will remember always what she had done for us, representing the worthy, noble and gallant English.

(Signed)
Lubbe, Willy
Interpreter Glyn Hughes Hospital
Belsen, Camp, 18th September 1945

The tragedy of Willi Lubbe is that sometime later he became mentally ill, and after causing a good deal of disturbance in the village in his endeavour to destroy the last SS man, the British Army Authorities placed him in a German mental asylum and we do not know his fate. It seems too awful that he is again in ruthless German clutches, whatever his political views.

I took a day off and went to Lübeck last week. The ambulance on the front seat of which I travelled was bound for various places, taking DPs who were looking for relatives. We drove round Hamburg looking for the Swedish Kirk and in so doing passed through a different part of the city to that which I had previously seen. The warehouse region on the canals was completely devastated, whole blocks of buildings drunkenly disgorging their interiors into the canal, and enormous piles of rubble not yet cleared away. I thought of Lenka and the other girls. Then we drove through the outer suburbs with leafy gardens and attractive houses, and through a pretty little village called Oldsloe and on to the Autobahn for twelve miles. We passed a British car and vehicle park, all wired off. The trucks and cars were packed side by side all the way. I've never seen so many, probably being collected from all over the British area and mostly in very good condition and no longer required by the Army. Another section of the Autobahn was similarly turned into an enormous petrol dump. Lübeck was considerably damaged, but some attractive old buildings still stand. We saw huge food queues, but the shop windows were practically empty. We left Belsen at 8.30 am in clear, sunny, crisp weather and arrived back at 7.30 pm.

Two of my German nurses were arrested the day before yesterday by our Security Officers as a number of patients were dissatisfied with the nursing they received from them, and signed statements to the effect that they had made anti-British remarks and that one has stated that 'she had been a Nazi, was a Nazi and always would be a Nazi'. The German Matron nearly had a stroke when I told her they were to pack up and be ready for the guard at 5 pm. Off they marched and are now in jail and will shortly be transferred to Hamburg. I hope it will have a salutary effect on the rest of the staff!

Later

Today is Sunday 30th September and I have just finished an uninterrupted round and spoken to every patient. Progress was slow; so many requested shoes, clothes, tooth-brushes and tooth paste, a routine cry these days. They love to talk and tell you '*Keine Kleider, keine Schuen, jeine Zahnpaste,*' ('No clothes, no shoes, no toothpaste'), and show you their little bits of treasures. They are working very hard for an Exhibition of their handcrafts next week. It is wonderful what they can improvise—embroidery done with coloured threads drawn from old towels and rings, and brooches made from the tick mica windows of planes. They arrange artistic dishes of moss, toadstools and autumn leaves on their bedside lockers, and decorate their wards with sprays of branches of greenery.

We have had a good deal of trouble with the recent cut in rations. Although the calories are adequate, the diet lacks variety and the bulk they so dearly love—many a time we have had to tactfully quell an argument or protest lodged by half the ward, out of bed and chattering in the excitable Continental way.

We have, with great difficulty, managed to obtain one pint of raw milk for each of our Tb patients daily. Since this milk was available, much cheese-making has taken place. Each bed, door knob and water-tap in the ward has its muslin bag suspended and filled with the precious milk, which they keep until sour and then leave so that the buttermilk will ooze through and drip either onto the floor or into a jar conveniently placed, according to the standards of the individual. They love it, the sourer the better; they call it *Quark*. Now what would you do? Have the cheese made in the kitchen, deprive them of much joy and interest but at the same time produce a healthier, easier and cleaner ward? See what you could do to persuade them to drink the nice sweet raw milk, and probably die of frustration and a broken heart in the process? Smile encouragingly, overlook the drips, ignore the quantities of jars full of smelly souring milk placed on every available chair or table, and admire the juicy bags of cream cheese and die happy? I am doing the latter, for the time being anyway.

The Head burst in today; her visits are never very satisfactory, always in too much of a hurry to give one a chance to discuss problems. Things must be pretty serious, I think, as UNRRA's plans have been changed and an agreement is to be signed with the Army next week. All very hush, hush but it was hinted that we may have greater responsibilities with the German population (bombed-out and displaced), and leave the DPs to be nursed in German hospitals.

Can you imagine anything more cruel? I mentioned that I doubted whether the staff would agree to this, as it was not the work they'd come to do—she said it was probably what we'd have to do—so I reserved my opinion on that and said no more!

This letter is untidy and meandering but the best I can do under present circumstances. So please excuse. I read tonight in one of the few up-to-date papers we see that the Japs are not as subdued as we would like and that we are landing troops in Java, etc. Don't you believe that the Germans are beaten either—and if anyone ever tells you that the only Nazi you can trust is a dead one, he is probably correct.

You will notice from this letter the name of the Camp has been changed from Belsen to Hohne—a tiny village nearby. Psychologically this is a very good move, particularly as so many DPs who were never in Belsen Concentration Camp are coming in at present.

We lost our housekeeper the week after she arrived—no loss really because she did no work at all and was very disagreeable about her posting to Belsen.

7th October 1945

The autumn tints are lovely now—crimson and golden maples and birches, and red squirrels among the carpet of russet leaves. Today is cold and bleak and so dark that I was forced to light my baby lantern at 4 pm.

The cheese making in the wards still flourishes but the smell was so bad yesterday that I reluctantly had to stop it—those who prefer *Quark* in preference to raw milk will have it made in the kitchen in future. I hated having to take this bit of pleasure from them but the sky's the limit and the wards smelt to high heaven!

We hear that the Russians are driving the Germans out of Poland, Czechoslovakia and the Eastern European States at half an hour's notice—they say thousands are dying on the way and in the trucks on arrival in Berlin.

Evidently, the tables have turned and the Dictatorship, with all its horrors, is working the other way now. Anyway, what's in a name? From what I can gather, Nazism and Communism are much the same in principle and practice.

My hands are so cold I can scarcely hold the pen so must conclude this epistle.

CHAPTER 8

THE LUNEBERG TRIALS

F. Tannenbaum, 'Life in Concentration Camp' series, Belsen, 1945

Hohne Assembly Centre
10th October 1945

This is to give you a description of the day I spent in Luneberg, at the trial of the War Criminals associated with Belsen and Auschwitz concentration camps. The trials began on 17th September and will probably continue for some time, as progress is slow owing to the necessity for translating the whole procedure into so many languages.

Three of us set out from Belsen at 7.30 am on 1st October in the UNRRA station wagon, each provided with a thermos of tea and sandwiches. It was rather dull when we left, but soon the day turned to one of autumn crispness and warm sunshine. The countryside was lovely—the trees are turning crimson and gold and for long distances meet in an archway overhead.

We arrived in Luneberg at 9 am, parked the wagon and walked across to the British Military Court House, which was barricaded off and guarded by armed British sentries in their red caps. Our official passes appeared to satisfy them and we were allowed to pass on to the main entrance, where they again produced the open sesame. We were shown into very good seats behind the witness box and had time to survey the court before the day's session opened.

This rough diagram will give you some idea of the positions:

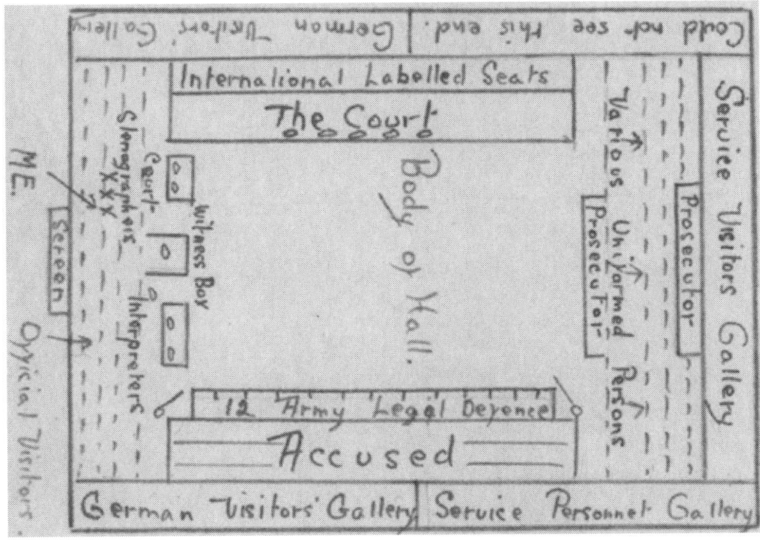

German carpenters had converted a gymnasium into a court-house to hold 250 of the public as well as the officials. The public gallery facing the accused was crowded with Germans who were listening to the revelations of the Concentration Camps with rapt attention. This gallery was closed in with wire netting. Some of these people, although Germans, had suffered under the Hitler regime. All Germans were searched before they entered the court and pocket knives, etc., removed in case they attempt to pass them for the prisoners to commit suicide. The German press was represented by nine men and I believe news of the trials is being given over the Hamburg Radio.

Seated in three-tiered rows, with the most notorious in the front, the prisoners were guarded by men and women of the British Military Police. There were forty-five prisoners in the dock, twenty-six men and nineteen women. I think three others on trial were ill and did not attend, because I saw one wearing No. 48. They were dressed either in old SS uniforms without badges or as civilians, and were the most menacing and degenerate-looking lot of human beings I've ever seen together. Obviously with a poor mental development. They filed in, some smirking, others stolid and sullen, and took their seats. Large black numbers on a white background were sewn on the backs of their garments and on cardboard hung round their necks in front. It is said that each of these accused is responsible for at least 1000 murders.

No. 1 was Kramer, the Beast of Belsen, a grim, thin-lipped heavy creature with narrowly set eyes, low and receding forehead and dark hair. He showed no emotion during the trial but scribbled notes from time to time.

No. 2, Dr Klein, sat next to Kramer and was a more wiry type with a head which appeared to have been squashed up on both sides and surmounted with tufted greying hair. He was the Mad Doctor of Belsen and described the place as a camp of death, I believe.

No. 9, 21-year-old Irma Grese, looked rather defiant, a pert young thing with eyes of steel, very little chin and a straight, small, hard, cruel mouth. She appeared amused at the proceedings and admitted that she had used whips made of tough, transparent, twisted paper on helpless women.

No. 6, Juana Bormann, was the woman who had the savage

dog which, when she let it loose on the prisoners, tore them to pieces. She was a wicked-looking witch and religious fanatic about forty years old, small, thin and sallow, or rather, prune-coloured.

Elizabeth Volkenrath, whom I think was No. 11 but am not quite sure, is about twenty-six years old and is alleged to have beaten seven people to death with a truncheon—she was known as the Jew Gasser.

One would imagine that all these prisoners must have been mentally unstable in some way. They say many of the SS were chosen from the bullies and degenerates at school. The men looked like some of the worst characters from the Rogues Gallery at Madame Tussauds—many of the women had small square chins and little hard mouths and assumed an insolent attitude. Irma Grese had worked in concentration camps since she was seventeen and said she liked it. It was an experience, and it will be interesting to see the result of the trial. I believe Kramer was in the box yesterday, the 9th October 1945, and his wife and Dr Klein today. The defence those 'innocents' put up is amazing, but Dr Klein let Kramer down today—so there is apparently no honour among thieves when their necks are in the noose. I took notes at the trial but am afraid I may not have got all the names correctly spelt.

The day I was there at 9.10 am, after an announcement was made in English and German that all were to be seated within the next ten minutes, the prisoners filed in at 9.20 am. All persons were seated and were instructed to keep their hats on until the Court entered. Punctually, the Court entered and we stood until the President, Major General H. P. M. Bernay-Ficklin CB, MC, crisply instructed all to be reseated.

A civilian member of the Judge Advocate-General's Branch, Mr C. L. Stirling, gave the court expert advice on all legal points. The first witness was a Rumanian doctor, Sigismund Charles Bendel, who gave his evidence in French and who was excellent and could not be shaken. He looked a worn and broken man and had come from Paris for the trial; he was arrested by the Nazis because he was not wearing the compulsory Jewish Star. The interpreting was excellent. The Prosecutor, Colonel T. M. Backhouse, an English Barrister and Field Marshall Sir Bernard Montgomery's Assistant Judge Advocate-General, put the questions in English, they were translated into French, the doctor replied in French, which was in turn translated to English for the Court and German and Polish for the accused. This is the story he told:

On 10th December 1943, Dr Bendel was sent to Auschwitz concentration Camp in Poland and at first was forced to work as a stone mason and later as a doctor to a Gypsy camp of 11 000, where he saw injections causing instantaneous death given as experiments to men, women and children. By July 1944, 4300 of these prisoners had gone to the Crematorium, and except for a working party of 1500, all others had died.

In June 1944, he stated, an SS doctor had 'given him the honour' by attaching him to the Crematorium. He was asked if he worked in the crematorium and stated that he and 900 other deported persons called the Special Kommando were forced to work there. There were also Senior Kommandos who were given special privileges and who lived completely separate from the other SS guards. There were about fifteen of these special men, three for each crematorium.

The DP special Kommandos were locked in special Blocks when not working and were not allowed to leave. The German SS guards were relieved by other German SS men. There were four crematoria, each equipped with two gas chambers, at Auschwitz. The witness lived first as a DP in camp and then at the crematorium itself. In August 1944, on his first day, 150 political prisoners, Russians and Poles, were led out one by one and shot, but no one was cremated. Two days later he saw the crematorium working. He was on day duty (there was a night shift also). In the Ghetto were 80 000 people. At 7 am the white smoke was still rising from the last of those who had been incinerated during the night.

This method was much too slow for the numbers to be cremated, so three large trenches about 17 × 6 yards were dug and the bodies were finished off with wood fires, saturated with petrol. This also was too slow, so canals were built in the centre of the trenches into which the human fat dropped and burning was hastened. Dr Bendel said the capacity of the trenches was almost fantastic. Where No. 4 crematorium had been able to burn 1000 persons daily, the trenches were able to cope with this number in one hour.

Transports were arriving with between 800 to 1000 people daily.

Those too ill to walk would be in tip-trucks, from which, to the amusement of the drivers, they were spilled without warning.

He was asked by the prosecutor to describe a day's work. His description is as follows:

> At 11 am the chief of the political Department arrived on a motor bike to announce that a new transport was expected. The trenches had to be prepared, cleaned out, and wood for burning and petrol put in. At 12 midday the new transports arrived, 800 to 1000 people, who were undressed in the courtyard and promised a bath followed by hot coffee. They were ordered to put their clothes on one side and valuables on the other. They entered a big hall where they had to wait until the gas arrived. In winter they undressed in this hall. Five to ten minutes later the gas arrived in a Red Cross ambulance, the strongest insult to a Doctor and the Red Cross.
>
> The doors of the two gas chambers were opened and the people sent in—terribly crowded. One had the impression that the roof was falling on their heads, the ceiling was so low. Forced in by blows from whips and sticks, they were not allowed to retreat—when they realised that it was death which they were facing they tried to return to the hall, but the SS guards finally succeeded in locking the doors. There were cries, shouts, fighting, kicking on the walls for two minutes, then nothing more.

This moment in the court was tense, the doctor spoke so quietly but with such dignity and conviction that we were all aghast at what we knew was the stark and awful truth.

> Five minutes later the doors were opened but it was impossible to go near the gas chamber. Twenty minutes later the special Kommandos started to work. Doors were opened, bodies fell out, quite contracted—it was impossible to separate one from the other. One gained the impression that they had fought terribly against death. Anyone who has seen a gas chamber filled to a height of four feet with corpses will never forget it. At this moment the special Kommandos stopped. They then took out the bodies, still warm, covered with blood and excrement. Before being thrown into the ditches they passed into the hands of the barber and the dentist. The hair was used by the Germans to make material. The teeth contained much precious metal and also did not burn easily.
>
> Now proper hell is started. The Kommandos are told to

> work as fast as possible—they try to drag the corpses by the wrists in furious haste—they worked like devils, they were no longer like human beings as they dragged the corpses away under a rain of blows. A barrister from Salonika, an electrical engineer from Budapest. Three to six SS men gave blows from rubber truncheons and continued to shoot people in front of the trenches, people who could not be put into the gas chambers because they were so overcrowded. After an hour and a half the work was done. The newest transport had been dealt with in crematorium No. 4.

Asked who had been the commandant at Auschwitz at the time, Dr Bendel quickly replied, 'Kramer. Commandant Kramer was in charge at this camp and was seen at the crematorium several times and was present at the killings.' (I have since been told that he used to gloat over this.) On one occasion a man who worked at the crematorium tried to escape, was brought back and killed. SS doctors were seen at the crematoria, and one Dr Klein (in court) was seen in the ambulance which brought the gas, sitting next to the driver.

> On 7th October 1944, 300 special DP Kommandos were told they were to work elsewhere, but they knew they were going to their death. That day 500 people (400 in Crematorium No. 3 and one hundred in Crematorium No. 1) were killed. The DP Kommandos were killed in No. 3. They were called one by one, undressed naked, put in rows of five, and an SS man passed by and shot them in the neck.

As a doctor, the witness had to attend to any of the Kommandos if they had an accident, such as burning human fat on their feet.

'In December 1944,' he continued, 'at Auschwitz four women were hanged in the women's compound for passing dynamite to a doctor for the purpose of exploding the camp—the girls worked in a munitions factory and were publicly hanged without trial. Hoessler ordered the hanging.' The witness was asked to identify anyone and he picked out Kramer and Dr Klein. He had never seen Hoessler, who was also present, he said.

The senior doctor at Auschwitz, a Dr Mengele, carried out human experiments, but no DPs took part in any of these. H. P. Feuhrer Moll gave the orders and Moll was responsible to Kramer, who received his instructions from the Political Department of which Himmler was chief.

On 7th October 1944, crematorium No. 3 was set on fire by the DPs there, 500 people took part in the revolt, but owing to some confusion and misunderstanding they could not reach their firearms.

The Court adjourned at 11.40 am for ten minutes. At 12 noon the second witness was sworn in: a Jew from Lodz, Poland, Romason Polanski by name (not sure of spelling). He was arrested in 1939 because he was a Jew, and was in a number of camps including Auschwitz in the autumn, 1943. When the Russians were advancing in the east, he was removed to Belsen. He was asked to identify any of the accused, who were floodlit for the purpose. He identified Kramer, Hoessler, Schlamontz, and a Pole named Ambon. 'My good friend,' as he put it and whose name he did not know but who was in the stores at Belsen.

Asked what Kramer had done, he stated that three days before the liberation of Belsen, witness went to the cookhouse and there were rotten potatoes lying on the ground. He started picking these up (they had been starving, you will remember), when Kramer shot his two friends dead and wounded him in the hand. He passed round the court and he exhibited the wound. Asked about the *man in the stores* he said he had led the men who had dragged the corpses to the graves and beat people with rifle butts and shot them when too exhausted to work. He also bit and kicked them. He hid himself and shot the starving prisoners as they tried to find food. They were all killed as he was only two or three metres away.

Hoessler, he said, was Commandant of No. 1 Crematorium at Auschwitz. In 1943, on their arrival at the railway station, Hoessler approached and formed them in fives. The witness said he tried to stay with his two brothers, but Hoessler sent them to the crematorium. He (the witness) worked there himself later, employed in cleaning the gas chambers and loading dead bodies onto lorries.

The Court adjourned at 1.15 pm and resumed at 2.30 pm. During this interval we sat in the station wagon and ate our lunch.

The previous witness again entered the box for a brief period and then the third witness appeared: Anita Loske, a German Jewess of Breslau, imprisoned in Auschwitz, December 1943, as a political prisoner. She actually saw selections being made by Hoessler and Dr Klein of hospital patients destined for the gas chamber. She said people were lined up at these selections and marched by—those who were to live were put on one side, those destined for the gas chamber on the other. This girl was a member of the Band which played at these selections and at public hangings in the camp. She was later transferred to Belsen.

Some days before the British arrived, Red Cross armbands were issued to workers by Dr Klein and they were told to be kind, etc. The approach of the British also affected the SS women, who pretended to be interested in the prisoners' welfare. Prisoners were told to be very strong because they were to be liberated soon. Previously these women, including Irma Grese, had carried whips and treated them very badly.

Three days before the arrival of the British all prisoners were assembled by Kramer and told to start digging graves, into which they had to drag the bodies. She identified Kramer, Dr Klein, Hoessler, Grese and others, and when she had finished giving evidence, stood for fully three minutes, just looking at them in silence. What a moment of triumph! She said later that the existence of the gas chambers was well known.

In answer to a question, she said the Hungarians came to Auschwitz Camp in May 1944. There were queues waiting day and night for cremation as there were so many people. She was taken to Belsen in November 1944, when there were very few people there and no huts; they lived in tents. Conditions were bad; it was winter, they were sick and had to wash outside in the cold and rain. The SS beat the inmates to keep order. Kramer arrived at Belsen about December 1944, and conditions became worse—beatings and other cruelties were introduced. There was no orchestra at Belsen. She was beaten with wooden sticks in Belsen for being late.

The fourth witness came in at 4 pm, but before she entered, all numbers were removed from the prisoners and No. 22 was allowed to change his place to wherever he liked.

The fourth witness was a girl of twenty-one, a Polish Jewess from Warsaw, arrested in April 1943 and sent to Auschwitz for sixteen or seventeen months, and to Belsen in July or August 1944. In Auschwitz her mother was with her, but was taken to the bathroom, beaten by SS women with a stick and issued with prison clothes, but she knew she was destined for the gas chamber. She was asked to identify the women who had done this. No. 6 she said was one, and that everyone was frightened of her as she kept a savage dog. No. 7 was women's Camp Commander at Belsen and very cruel. No. 9, Irma Grese, carried and used a whip and also shot people. No. 10 was another. No. 11 collaborated with the SS in Camp No. 40, ill-treating hungry people, beating them kneeling down, etc., in winter. No. 48 was a notorious collaborator with the SS—everyone was frightened of her. And so on. No emotion was seen on these sadistic women's faces during this identification.

Witness No. 5, a Polish Jew, entered the box at 4.30 pm. He was arrested in 1941. He recognised No. 19 as being in charge of the transport which brought him from Dora Camp to Belsen. He had also been in Buchenwald. They had no food or water on the journey and when witness asked for the latter he was told he would get it with this pistol. The journey took seven days. More than fifty per cent died, bodies were left in the wagon on arrival at Belsen. No. 19 was walking along the train and was asked for water, which he refused. His attention was drawn to the bodies taking up space. It was suggested that they be thrown away, but he said that the others were going to die anyway so what was the difference. On arrival at Belsen they lay in the open and were beaten with iron bars. The witness' friend ended up in bed as a result of these beatings. The only reason for this treatment was that they were Jews. His friend died.

The accused was grinning during this evidence, and did not appear to attach any seriousness to it. I believe the accused prisoners are confined in the town jail, where two share a room fitted with running water and mirrors for the women. Their diet consists of a daily ration of one thick slice of German bread for breakfast, one litre of soup at midday, another slice of bread with corned meat and about half an ounce of margarine for supper. With each meal they receive a small can of ersatz coffee.

On 18th September Brigadier H. L. Glyn Hughes, the first witness in the trials, said, 'I have seen all the horrors of war, but I have never seen anything to touch Belsen.' He said that the expectancy of life for a person in reasonable health interned in Belsen Camp was no more than three months. When he toured the camp with the camp doctor, Klein, the latter appeared quite callous and indifferent.

Colonel Backhouse, who opened the prosecution, was frequently compelled to admit that no words could describe the horrible things which had occurred—and said before the Nazis came, mankind had no need of words to speak of such things. He said the women guards had found sport in setting wolf-hounds to tear living people apart. He also stated that the real horror was not the things he had been describing, but the fact that there existed in the German mind determination to inflict these horrors on fellow human beings.

The charge against all defendants is 'At Bergen-Belsen Germany, between 1st October 1942, and 30th April 1945, in violation of the law and usage of war, they were together concerned as parties to the ill treatment of certain persons, causing their deaths.' Thirteen Allied nationals who died are named, including a former member of the Royal Navy, Keith Meyer. The second charge against Kramer and eleven others is a similar charge concerning Auschwitz Concentration Camp, Poland.

Harold le Deuillence, the British survivor of Belsen, said he was having his first meal for five days when the British came—he was eating grass.

The Court adjourned at 5 pm and we had a comfortable drive back. That these men are given British justice is too fantastic and I'm sure they do not appreciate the privilege. I don't know how the twelve men for the defence can possibly do it, but, of course, they must, if selected, as they are all British army officials, except one Polish Lieutenant who is defending four of the Poles among the accused. Major T. C. M. Winwood defended Kramer, who with the other accused refused an opportunity to have German civilian counsel, whom they would have had to pay.

Well, my friends, this ghastly letter has been written in two sessions and is, I am afraid, rather disjointed, but will give you a first-hand picture of what a Totalitarian Dictatorship means for the world.

Chapter 9

OCCUPATIONAL THERAPY: A SPY, THERMOMETERS AND OTHER THINGS

F. Tannenbaum, 'Life in Concentration Camp' series, Belsen, 1945

C/- 168 Military Government Attachment
BAOR (British Army of the Rhine)
Hohne Assembly Centre
24th October 1945

On my return to Belsen I received an invitation from *Les Représentants du Clerge Catholique à Belsen* to a *Cérémonie Religieuse Catholique* to be held in Camp 1 on 2nd November *en la commémoration de tous le Fidèles Trepasses à la mémoire de tous ceux qui reposent ici et de tous ceux qui a leur exemple not donne leur vie pour la même et noble cause.* With this came also an invitation from the Polish Committee to attend an unveiling ceremony following the Mass, when a cross and graves will be consecrated.

I heard today that the Polish midwife in the old Maternity block had three sons, all of whom were deported by the Germans. She has no knowledge of where two of them are but the third arrived here last week, much to her joy. He had traced his mother from the lists of missing which are circulated in all the camps and hospitals. Such terribly long lists and so many names never crossed off. This time there was great rejoicing in one family, for the mother is no longer alone in the world.

Great preparations have been going on for the last few weeks for the three-day exhibition of patients' work organised by the occupational therapy department, which consists of a little group of untiring workers, former inmates of the Horror Camp. The welfare worker from the Vatican Mission to Belsen, and the UNRRA officer of the Welfare and Rehabilitation Department supervised it. We lent them our common room in the hospital and the result was a remarkable demonstration of what people can do with patience, ingenuity and a few bits and pieces.

It has been a joy to watch the enthusiastic efforts of the patients on my rounds of the wards. Practically all the articles were made by the victims of the concentration camps, now recovering from their experiences and starting life afresh. Some had been prisoners for periods varying from one to ten years. I was invited to act as hostess when the Brigadier from the 43rd Division (Wessex) and other high-ranking officials attended the opening on Friday 5th October.

There were leather belts, gloves and bags; baby garments and pullovers knitted from unravelled cream woollen German abdominal belts. Other belts and bags were made from a kind of twisted cellophane found in the Wehrmacht stores and recognised by some of the patients as materials they had been forced to make when imprisoned in Auschwitz extermination camp. They told me it was used to replace army webbing, and for whips which the SS women used on the prisoners.

There were stuffed elephants, deer and dogs with the quaintest expressions, and rings and brooches made from the perspex from aeroplane observation blisters. Men as well as women were exhibitors and some attractive wooden toys had been cunningly fashioned with the crudest tools and paints by the men.

Some of the women had collected old bits of grey blanket issued to the German workers for cleaning materials, and had made some really practical embroidered gloves and slippers from them. One little Hungarian Jewess, aged fifteen years, who is a genius with her fingers, had among a large collection of her work some dolls dressed in the original garments issued by the Germans to the women prisoners—the horrible dark blue and grey striped materials we now see as pyjamas and dressing gowns in hospital. This girl also dressed other dolls as gypsy fortune-tellers, complete with playing cards.

Tannenbaum displayed the series of his crayon drawings depicting events in the concentration camps, and the whole exhibition was a huge success. We hear it is to be taken to Paris and London and only hope that the things which we have bought are finally returned to us in good condition at Belsen.

We had a patient here recently calling himself a Spaniard who said he was an engineer-draughtsman. He was always most friendly and polite and wanted to join UNRRA. As we only have an old German, Herr Kitler (whom I frequently find myself addressing as Hitler), who acts as house steward, the SMO thought it would be quite a good idea to have an engineer on the premises who could attend to the hundred and one odd things which go wrong every day. Alas! Our Spaniard was arrested today as a spy!

Our twins born yesterday weighed less than 2 kg (2.2lbs) each, and one died this evening. The mother had been terribly ill and had suffered at the hands of the Germans before liberation, so we were not surprised that the babies were so delicate.

Souvenirs made and presented to Miss Doherty by some of the patients at the hospital at Belsen. The doll at the top is dressed in a prisoner's uniform, identical with the uniforms originally issued to prisoners by the Nazis, and made from the same material. The doll at the bottom is a gypsy fortune-teller, made from scraps by a Jewish girl of fifteen years whose eyesight was very poor.

We had some trouble with two German nurses again today. The patients in one ward reported them for anti-British outbursts. Christa Shiffman, a third-year medical student now acting as a Nurse help, had told the patients that 'of course they expected the British to come laden with gold, but that they had nothing to give the DPs and never would have anything to give them'. She pointed out that even the clothes they wore and medicines the doctors gave them were German, and so on! Clever, but not quite clever enough, for the patients are most appreciative of what the British have done and are doing for them, and are alert to German tricks and propaganda. The second, Nurse Lucia Hartmann, had declared her firm adherence to the Nazi Party a little too vehemently!

The Security Officers interviewed the patients, who also complained they were not receiving proper nursing care from these women. We collected some of those precious commodities—paper, pen and ink—for the written statements and then followed the usual procedure of notifying the German Matron that they were to pack their bags and be ready to leave in half an hour. These little interruptions all take time, but seem to be part of the business.

One of our German doctors, the German dentist Dr Kluzer, and the chief dispenser who is Dutch were arrested the other day. We are told they lose citizenship, possessions and profession. It had been revealed that the dispenser is a Dutch Nazi, who will be returned to Holland to be dealt with there. We disliked him and always felt there was something queer about him when he told us he wished to remain at Belsen in preference to returning to his own country, where he had a wife and four children of whom he was always talking!

I am sure there are many ardent Nazis here only waiting until the time is ripe to work once more for the Fatherland. A new underground movement had just been unearthed in this Zone, *Deustchland für die Deutschen*—Germany for the Germans—their aim being to force the British Army of Occupation out. I can see subtle moves even among the German personnel here, with occasional patriotic outbursts such as I have described.

A Hungarian Dance Band played in the main hospital corridor today and the beautiful music was relayed to the wards through the microphone system which has just been fixed up. The patients were thrilled and were out of bed dancing and pirouetting round.

The ground this week has been untidy, with fallen leaves everywhere, bare trees, and autumn beauty gone. It is colder too. We have had a little heating in the hospital and for a short time in the evening in the mess. How long this will continue depends on the coal supply, which is very low in this district, and transport from the mines is very scarce.

They say we are losing Monty and I did so want to see him!

Huntin', fishin' and shootin' seem to be the order of the day round here, mostly the latter when Pole meets German, or vice versa! The DP victims are, of course, admitted to hospital here but not the Germans. However, today a German who was working in the camp was shot through the eye and had been admitted. I don't like this because the German nurses give him all the attention at the expense of the other patients. I found them cooking all kinds of delicacies the other day, assisted by a German patient's wife and daughter, but nary a morsel were they giving to several very sick men in the same ward. This letter seems to be full of news about the Germans but I thought you might be interested.

That reminds me of another episode. Three times recently a German woman professing to have been a former occupant of one of our flats has called at the mess, demanding her furniture. On each occasion she was referred to me, but I soon dismissed her. How did we know that anything she might claim had actually belonged to her, especially as the articles had been collected from several sources and had passed through many hands since the Germans had hastily left? The last time, she arrived armed with a signed paper from the Military Government authorities permitting her to take practically what she liked! My first reaction was to ring the officer concerned, but on second thought I decided to try a bit of bluff and sent her about her business. We have not seen anything of her since, nor have I been reprimanded for not carrying out the Military Government instructions. The German audacity is almost beyond comprehension!

Did I tell you we had great difficulty in evicting some of the permanent residents of the old maternity block? We are taking over this and the old childrens' hospital as isolation wards and for emergency hospitals in the event of an epidemic, and are transferring the present occupants to other quarters which the authorities have provided for them. Mala, a Lithuanian girl, finally left, taking with her a complete set of bedroom furniture, electric light bulb (almost unprocurable at present) and rations for sixteen!

Whilst in London at the Investiture [where Muriel Doherty was awarded the Royal Red Cross, First Class] I was asked to make a broadcast on the BBC Pacific Service. At the conclusion of my talk, Richard Dimbleby, who spoke with me, gave a description of Camp No. 1 as he saw it at the time of liberation by the British. The BBC have just sent me my scripts, and I shall quote his impressions. He says:

> I think one of the most awful things about it was the suddenness. No one had told us this was a concentration camp—we understood it was some sort of refugee centre where there was an epidemic. The enemy had agreed to surrender it intact and we had agreed to take it over, that was all.
>
> But, as I drove up the road through the woods in my jeep, there came from the trees a terribly sickly smell. I knew it at once—it was the old sweet smell of death and decay. There were signs by the roadside—TYPHUS—with some scared-looking Germans guarding them. Then, the gates of the camp, and the camp itself, just a scattered, shapeless collection of huts, wired in.
>
> Brigadier Glyn Hughes, then the chief doctor of the 2nd Army, who has since been a witness at the trial, met me at the gate and took me in. He'd been there a few hours, but I think I was the first outside observer. He said, 'I hope you've got a strong stomach, you're going to see something horrible!'
>
> We drove into the compound, and I saw, for the first time, the swaying, drifting mass of people that was to become one of the horrors of the world's history. I think I knew it at once—at any rate, I took hold of myself and said, Now, then, you make a note of everything, get all the details and don't do anything damn silly like being sick or passing out.
>
> Almost at once a man lurching along the track ahead of us turned half round and fell violently on his side. It's always rather a shock to see someone fall over, isn't it? I mean right over. We swerved round this man, and the Brigadier leaned out of the jeep to look at him. He said as he leaned out again, 'He's dead.' 'Dead?' I said. 'He can't be dead just like that.' Glyn Hughes looked at me with a distress in his eyes that you might almost have called agony. There are 10 000 people dying here, he said, and 10 000 dead.
>
> The first shock, the first realisation of the ghastly situation, was something of a bromide. I think I followed the Brigadier

round in a daze, stepping over bodies, going in and out of dark huts where in the stench of a pig-sty, human beings were dying with the bodies of those who'd died a week before them as mattresses. A woman clutched at my ankle, and the sudden thought of contamination brought me round. I looked down at her—her fingers were like old brown pencils, her face a stretched parchment, I think you could have rattled your knuckles on it like a drum. She was dying—she would be dead in thirty minutes. Glyn Hughes examined her wasted skeleton and looked at me. 'She's about twenty,' he said.

At that time it seemed unnecessary to put the camp guards on trial. Why not shoot them in front of the wretched people they've been torturing, and be done with it? Let it be known that there would be instant and drastic justice for anyone caught in such foul work as theirs.

But as the time has gone by, I've realised that a full-dress trial was right. Such crimes are too big and too grave to be expiated by a single shot of a firing squad. We must show in public the wickedness of such people and demonstrate that even in cases as extreme as this they are given a chance to prove themselves innocent. However much people may grumble at the time it takes and the money it costs, the fact remains that when the Luneberg trial is over and the verdicts are given, the whole world will have been able to know—not in passion, but in cold proven legal detail—exactly what can happen behind the frontiers of a country that surrenders its soul to a dictator.

Meanwhile, we can take comfort from the fact that skill and, above all, humanity have made a wonderful job of the casualties of Belsen—right from that first day when Brigadier Glyn Hughes went into camp alone. Now at Belsen there's a first-class hospital—the hospital of which Miss Doherty has spoken. While the Luneberg trial condemns those who did the wrong, the Matron and her Sisters in the new Belsen are showing what kindness can do.

Hohne Assembly Centre
3rd November 1945

The Roman Catholic memorial service and unveiling of the cross took place yesterday. The day was dismal, with drizzling rain which made the camp look even more desolate than when I had visited it before. Thousands of Poles marched from Camps 2 and 3 in what appeared to be an endless procession. Polish Girl Guides and Boy Scouts in their cleverly improvised uniforms and tiny children carrying wreaths took part also. A Polish band played Chopin's funeral march and a very good choir sang an old Polish suppliant hymn.

We all congregated near the huge mass graves where a tall wooden memorial cross had been erected. The improvised altar was backed by British, American and Polish flags. The officiating priest had been imprisoned in the Horror Camp and was later a patient in the Glyn Hughes Hospital. Although his face still bore marks of his terrible experiences he had put on weight and looked much better.

The ceremony was rather too long for these people, many of whom are still poorly, and a number of children fainted during the long one and a half hours' service. The address was given from one of the nearby German observation towers, where so recently the vicious SS men had carried out target practice on the unfortunate and unprotected inmates.

From the papers we see that the Japanese are causing some trouble. It is the same with the Germans, no actual open warfare, but passive resistance all the time. Europe seems to be in a turmoil and full of confused ideas. We cannot see any solution at present. The Jews are growing impatient and it looks as if there would be trouble with the Arabs if they insist on returning to Palestine. Before I arrived here I wondered what my attitude towards the German nurses would be. Even if I felt hostile and bitter, to display my feelings would not produce the best treatment for our patients. On the other hand their servility, apparent friendship and excessive willingness was sometimes repulsive and did not always ring true. I felt it was part of the German policy, shall we say, towards the occupation authorities, especially noticeable when guns were in evidence, and that they were probably ridiculing the British generosity and reasonableness behind our backs.

I subsequently, after much thought, decided to accept them at their face value, deal with situations as they arose and adopt a normal but not too friendly attitude. I always feel, however, that they will adhere to their Nazi ideals and develop their anti-British underground movement as opportunity allows.

I am still at my wit's end to know where we can get some clinical thermometers. We have none in stock and only two for our eighty-seven patients with open pulmonary Tb. The central Europeans seem to be used to having their temperature taken in the axilla, and some actually are afraid of having the thermometer in their mouth. This, of course, does not make it any easier. The Army stores cannot produce any and our Quartermaster has been unable to find even one during his scouting round the country. I requisitioned for 144 recently, the SMO cut it to forty-eight and the Army authorities to twenty-four because as a DP Hospital we should not require as many as an Army Hospital!

The German matron thought she might be able to get a few from some undisclosed source, but after six weeks of waiting nothing has eventuated. Of course, we can get on without them, but it is much more satisfactory to have them when observing the patients' progress. Another problem which we are trying to solve is what to do with the patients' possessions, which at the moment in most of the wards clutter the beds, lockers, chairs and even the floor under the beds.

Some time ago, soon after my arrival actually, I had all the blackout curtains taken down and washed. Those that survived and were returned safely to the Glyn Hughes were to be made into bags which would tie on to the bed backs. You see, even if we had cupboards or store-rooms in which to put them away, the patients would not part with their precious and only possessions in the world. Their goods are tied up in old bits of carpet, blankets or hessian, are stuffed into old shabby battered bags and cases, or are just lying loose about their beds and surroundings. A large part of my time when doing rounds is taken up in inspecting and admiring many of these newly acquired treasures. We could not possibly destroy this joy by removing them to a central room, no matter how safe.

I engaged two German women to do the sewing in the small

room near my office in which we have now accumulated five sewing machines. Of course this was too easy to be true! We still only had one machine needle and no thread, and apparently none could be found in Germany! After considerable effort I procured a second needle and two precious reels of cotton and set the women to work. Several bags were made and distributed to one of the women's wards and things began to look a bit tidier. However, the output was much too slow so my assistant and I arranged to put our heads in the sewing room door every time we passed. You have no idea of the scuffling and shuffling of garments onto the seamstresses' laps when we entered. I think they must have been undertaking a private sewing business for all the Germans in the village. So we soon settled that!

Everyone is agog with the latest BBC news that unless America contributes her share UNRRA will not be able to continue. No one seems to know anything much at present, but we are waiting expectantly and wondering what the future holds.

There have been a series of conferences here recently and many delays over the introduction of the plan whereby UNRRA takes over the control of the entire camp and all the voluntary agencies working here, under the UNRRA umbrella. Up to date UNRRA has only been in charge of the hospital section.

It was hinted again the other day that we might be required to deal with the German sick and destitute instead of the DPs. We hear that plans are in the making for the Jews to take over the management of their sick, and other plans for the training of hospital aids to assist any trained nurses they might find among the displaced persons, who could take over the care of the Polish patients. I think there are similar plans for the Balts (for example, the Latvians, Lithuanians and Estonians) who refuse to return to their own country while it is under Soviet control.

Suggestions for the Nurses' Training Programme at Belsen (extract)

Purpose

1. To orientate the nurses to nursing care of DPs. Also health supervision of DPs.
2. To give practical instruction to fit the nurses for duty in the camp.

3. To give those without any public health training some knowledge of the fundamentals of public health.
4. To assess the professional ability and administrative capacity of the nurses and to determine the particular job for which each is best suited.

Outline of the Course

The course should include the following lectures and conferences:

1. General plan of UNRRA work with DPs in Germany.
2. Psychology of DPs. (This should be given by a psychiatrist or other psychiatric worker if such personnel is available, but it is essential they have some experience with the DPs.)
3. The Nurse in the Team—responsibility to: duties; uniform; department; reporting, etc.
4. Special conference and, when possible, demonstrate on child welfare, school, hygiene, midwifery.
5. Sanitation of the environment and the nurse's responsibility for this in the camp.
6. The Welfare Worker and the nurse. (This to be given jointly by a Welfare Worker and a nurse, bringing out the necessity for co-ordination of the Health and Welfare programmes.)
7. Directed observation trips about Belsen to see the camp, the welfare work, sanitation, etc.
8. Principles of public health for those who have not had any public health training or experience.

In view of this, I made enquiries as to how many trained nurses and hospitals aides there were in Belsen Camp. We had already tried unsuccessfully to find some to assist in our hospital. You see, after liberation everyone who could, when scarcely fit after their illness and starvation, had assisted with the nursing. Then, as opportunity occurred, they either returned to their own country or moved elsewhere.

My enquiry did not meet with much success for there were only seven trained nurses and they are already assisting the British Red Cross and St John's Ambulance workers in the medical inspection or, as we know them, first aid and treatment rooms in the camp. So I don't think we will be nursing the Germans after all. I think that is definitely the work of their own nurses, of whom there does not appear to be any shortage at present.

We had five murders in the nearby forest last night. All were

Germans shot through the head. Motive unknown. Murderers not yet captured. One is not surprised when one considers that all these people are herded together practically without occupation and that in all this tremendous European upheaval there must be some criminals at large, in addition to those people who have a very genuine grudge against their former captors.

My hands are very cold, we have no heating because the coal supply has given out. The Hospital was like a morgue today but, strangely, the original concentration camp patients do not seem to feel it nearly as much as we do. We see them wandering about in the scantiest of clothing, or sitting on their beds with their bare legs dangling with only a thin vest or nightdress on. Unfortunately, we only have a very limited number of dressing gowns, which we keep mainly for the men who are permitted to walk around.

My UNRRA staff has been reduced to eight including myself and I am at my wit's end to arrange the supervision, give them their proper time off duty and keep everyone contented. The local UNRRA HQ administration appears to have lost interest in us now that we are no longer in the news.

We heard over the air from Nuremburg Court Room that Hess, Ribbentrop, Goering, Raeder, Keitel, Schacht, Streicher the Jew Baiter, and others pleaded NOT GUILTY! Goering tripped over three pairs of feet when walking to the witness box to make the announcement on behalf of his fellow criminals!

We have some well-organised clinics now. Tuberculosis, ear, nose and throat, eye, gynaecological and ante- and post-natal; and we think our Mothers' Convalescent Home, to which our mothers and babies are transferred after ten days in the Maternity Hospital, is a model, especially the babies' bathroom and nursery.

I nearly forgot to tell you that I was godmother again on 4th November. The ceremony this time was in our Mothers' Convalescent Home. Three Polish babies, three godfathers and three godmothers, but no fathers. We all sat down to a feast afterwards—black coffee from ward mugs, and sweet cakes made by the mothers themselves. Mothers, babies, priests, godfathers and godmothers and I—all sat in the sitting-room we had just furnished and had a lovely time. My godchild's name this time is Krysstow (Christopher) Rund and he is five months old. He was a very sick baby in our hospital and the mother refused to leave him at one stage, terrified that the German nurses would not nurse him carefully. However, I managed to persuade her that Christopher was safe and the honour was subsequently bestowed on me.

Hohne
18th November 1945

It is sometime since I wrote you a decent letter, but I have been completely overwhelmed with work. A nasty form of tracheitis and influenza spread through and depleted my UNRRA nursing staff for a time. One Sister was very ill with acute oedema of the pharynx and soft palate, but recovered after being treated with Penicillin. For one night I wondered in my mind who could do a tracheotomy if necessary—we had no Surgeon on the staff at that time, except a German. I was very glad when she was transferred to the 29th British General Hospital in Hanover.

In the midst of this, three UNRRA nurses were posted and a week later two more. Sometimes it takes all one's courage not to be completely disheartened by the administration. Having got my staff (and myself) on their feet again, I received two new Dutch nurses, who would have been appreciated during the strenuous and anxious period when I had to use one of my few UNRRA nurses to nurse her colleague. It is rather exasperating when one hears from all sides that there are nurses itching for work and as many as ten at local HQ waiting for assignments, at the same time a nearby area supervisor saying she has more nurses than she knows what to do with! Perhaps I'm fussy.

This epistle will be a pot pourri, I'm afraid, with all the oddments of news I can think of. The glorious autumn colourings have gone, the trees are bare except the pines, spruce and a few others. We had one gloriously heavy fall of snow when all my childhood dreams came true—one could almost see the gnomes and fairies amid the sparkling crispness and snowy whiteness. The originators of the fairy tales could not have lacked inspiration in this part of the world. But what a mess when the snow began to melt, with mud and slush everywhere, and then it froze and the roads became dangerously glassy. We have since had some crisp, sunny days and on one of them I drove through the camp on my way to our Mothers' Convalescent Home.

What a contrast to six months ago! Today young men and women were gaily strolling along in holiday mood or leaning out of former barrack windows—the present home of the Belsen community of some 21 000—talking to their swains below. Others were arranging washing on grassy patches or stunted bushes, some even had clothes lines strung up with the weirdest collection of garments you could imagine.

When the British troops liberated Belsen, you will remember, they commandeered quantities of clothing from the surrounding districts at gun point; the Germans produced fairly good stuff and I think quite a lot came from warehouses and stores.

Later, when the local burgomaster was responsible for seeing that each German surrendered so many garments, the best stuff went underground, I think. You can hardly credit the result— Great-grandmother's undies of solid German proportions, all Auntie's old out-dated summer garments, and little Willie's cast-off shoes and cotton panties, often beyond recognition as clothing.

Of course, many of our DPs provided themselves with very good outfits by the process of organisation known locally as *Klipsi Klipsi*, and in some of the photos I sent you they look snugly and smartly clad. Blankets are still the bane of our lives, for our source of supply is dwindling and the wards are very cold owing to the shortage of coal, so that I am obliged to keep a close hold on those we have. We count and count, check and check, but never have the same number, nor sufficient.

On 8th November, six blankets were issued to A2, one of our men's surgical wards, to make up their numbers. On 9th November I told the Oberschwester to count the total in the ward, result showed 285. As the full bed state was sixty-eight and we allow three blankets per bed there should have been 204 in use, giving a surplus of eighty-one blankets. That sounded as if some borrowing had taken place and our deficit in other wards would now be erased. The blankets were re-checked to see how many patients had more than three—four patients claimed that the extra blankets found on their beds were their own property. That left us a total of 281 in the ward. In the afternoon the Oberschwester attempted to straighten out the question by seeing that each bed had only three hospital blankets. She reported that now she could count only 190 blankets, leaving a shortage of fourteen! She now claimed that when the issue had been made a month previously, A2 had received fifteen less than its correct amount. This was not the case, for I know that all wards received the correct number, but the Germans always have a ready excuse to cover themselves and she was a bit slow in thinking up that one. A1 and A5 were sixty-eight short and we thought that some blankets had been borrowed by A2. There was great joy therefore when the 281 were found, as those missing in A1 and A5 could be made up. However, this little matter was never completely clarified and we gave up counting. Do you ask, Can Jerrys count? However, that's nothing; I read in yesterday's paper that 500 000 army stock blankets are missing from Dumfries, so we cease to worry.

I was recently promised some very attractive mignonette green, satin-bound US blankets and some two-toned brown of the same kind by the Belsen Camp Stores. The next day I was offered an alternative of Khaki US Comforters (eiderdowns issued to troops) and I decided that the added attraction of the mignonette green wasn't worth the anxiety of preventing a scoop in the tailoring trade and the subsequent appearance of hundreds of Paris models, although I had been assured that anyone seen in garments of said blankets would be arrested. The comforters had it.

I now ask each patient to sign a list on the back of the treatment sheet, showing that he has received three blankets on loan, two sheets, one towel, and one pillow-case. Any brought in by the patients or their friends are also noted—but still they vanish and we know the Germans are not blameless.

So much for blankets; and we return to our drive round the camp, where children played and babes slept peacefully, blissfully ignorant of the many tragedies with which they were surrounded. Here and there we passed a group of gypsies, ever willing for one to cross the palm with cigarettes. Many people were chopping wood, gathering everything that would burn, from the roofs of the bicycle shelters of Nazi days to the wooden-slatted mattresses of their own bedsteads!

They still stroll through the spruce forests searching for some of the villainous-looking bright orange mushrooms which they consider such delicacies. At meal times one sees the inmates of the blocks queuing up for their cooked rations. Many still prefer to take them to their rooms and reconstruct, rather than eat them in the canteens. In the mornings great cauldrons of steaming food, porridge and soup are delivered at the doors of the blocks and it is interesting to see the individuals diving in with all kinds of ladles, arms immersed almost to the shoulder in the containers and hardly anyone replacing the lid!

Here is life for all; and to many, hope; and to some, a future. They are moderately comfortable with good food, clothing and warm beds, in quarters formerly occupied by the strutting Panzer guards. Only a short time ago there were picnics in the woods, moonlight walks, open-air dances, and there are still concerts, cinemas, costume plays, sports, love-makings, weddings and christenings.

There is uncertainty for many whose future is undetermined or who cannot or do not wish to return to their own countries for various reasons. The greatest tragedy is that of the Jews and Poles. The Jews, of course, cannot or do not wish to return to the countries from which they came. There is a tremendous move among them to return to Palestine—it is constantly being pressed at meetings, in plays, concerts and their daily life. After living among them, one understands their problems and one sympathises with them, even though we perhaps feel a little exasperated at times.

Many of their action plays and mannerisms savour of the East and I am sure some of them will never be happy again in the West. They are always having meetings of protest and only a few weeks ago staged a strike, with a procession and banners bearing the words 'Back to Palestine'.

The Poles are another problem—originally we either had Polish Jews, Poles from concentration camps and slave workers. They mostly refused to return to Poland under what they term Russian occupation, which some of them experienced early in the war when the Red Army marched into their country. The Soviet-dominated Communist Government in Poland is also turning out many of its own Jewish countrymen who find their way to this and other camps. Latterly we have had some thousands of volunteer labourers and their families who were enticed to work for the Germans and who, unless they can produce conclusive evidence to prove that they were compelled to enter Germany, tell us they will be and are being liquidated if they return to Russian-occupied Poland. They are all in the strict sense of the word DPs, but one cannot have the same sympathy for them as one does for victims of the concentration camps, although, unless they tell us, we do not know the difference, and as patients they are all the same to us, whatever their race, religion or political leanings.

Many of the young people here were thrust into concentration camps or forced from their countries as slave labourers at an early age, and yet they are full of courage, energy and enterprise. Frau Dr Kramer, our housekeeper, a doctor of philosophy in her own country and a charming little Jewess, was in Auschwitz with her husband, daughter and relatives. One day they were brought out for selection. Her husband, mother, sister and the sister's two young children were inspected and put on one side, her daughter Eva and herself on the other. She was told that her relatives were going to another camp but that she could see them on Sunday—Sunday came and she was told it would be the next week, and so on until finally some SS guard jeeringly told her that they had gone to the gas chamber and crematorium. Actually, her husband was sent to the terrible concentration camp at Dachau, where he died just at liberation and she received the news after she came to us. She and Eva, being young, strong and attractive, were put to work in a factory and so survived—Eva was seventeen years old today and was overcome when we all gave her presents. There was much kissing of hands (which is really most elegant when one grows accustomed to it) and she was very happy.

These young things are so ingenious with their hands and create some of the smartest models—such as our leading and most exclusive stores would envy. Unfortunately materials and equipment for their work are still in short supply and it is disappointing that, as a result, constructive occupation is not more developed.

When I commenced this letter we were driving through the camp, so let us continue as we pass a crocodile of children of all shapes and sizes making their way to the Tented Theatre for a rehearsal of the concert they are giving during the Jewish festival of Chanukkah. The growing adolescent girls are well nourished on the whole and have lovely skins and eyes. The boys are less well covered. Some of the younger ones show signs of malnutrition and are very thin.

We passed the HQ of the Central Jewish Committee bedecked with their colours, pale blue and white, with various inscriptions in Hebrew including the 'Back to Palestine' slogans. We passed the Kinderheim where some eighty unaccompanied displaced children;

German, Hungarian and Polish Jews, and a few gypsies have been assembled. Many of them were picked up by the RAF in Berlin and other districts, with no trace of relatives. They have a school daily and are learning Hebrew, Yiddish, and a number speak English. The Continentals pick up languages very quickly.

The children seem to lose their terror symptoms quickly in their new surroundings. They were hoping to go to England and were so excited and were all being medically examined and having their chests X-rayed. Switzerland was also taking some and about fifty went to Paris recently. There seems to be some hitch in the English and Swiss evacuation at present, much to our discomfort as we lent them, very temporarily, a building which we were to convert into a sixty-bed Isolation Ward and now we can't get it back! Although we have no control there (and we wish we had, for they badly need the supervision of a trained nurse) Dr Tewsley supervises their health.

On our way round the camp we passed the Swiss International Red Cross Team's offices, where they have a complete mobile X-ray unit and are endeavouring to microphotograph the chests of all in the camp! Alas, their efforts have not met with great success for many reasons. The Professor in charge told me that many of the people were still suspicious that it meant the gas chamber, and others were actually afraid of what the X-ray might reveal and of the subsequent curtailment of their activities through hospitalisation.

'Swan Lake' looked lovely today—our one swan flew away recently but returned a few days later without giving an explanation!

Passing the Round House, now occupied by an army unit, I was reminded of the days when it was packed with humanity suffering from advanced pulmonary Tb, and of the days before that when the Hitlerites with pomp and ceremony held their banquets and balls. The kitchens with their vast and modern equipment would make many a Hospital Matron envious and shake the Hospitals Commission of New South Wales to its foundations.

I noticed the Hohne Camp Stores have opened but did not enter, owing to the large queue waiting outside. This is one further step in rehabilitation because the DPs who are employed by the Military Government can purchase goods here with the money they earn. So you see, from liberation, the stages in rehabilitation have been:

1. Feeding, delousing, clothing, nursing and housing
2. Convalescence
3. Employment
4. Financial independence, and the appreciation of the value of money once more.

It is time to do rounds at the Mothers' Convalescent home now, so we alight. You will remember that this Home was the original Maternity Hospital, a rather grubby place conducted by a DP Rumanian doctor, with a Lithuanian dentist (female) as Oberschwester and a couple of Polish DP midwives! The doctor, I told you before, had been in Auschwitz and you can imagine how that experience must have affected her. When she left we took the Hospital over, but had a good deal of difficulty until we were able to dismiss the dentist and her assistant nurse (who took all the bedroom furniture and fittings with them) and inform the midwife that she could no longer have her son living with her in the hospital!

Then the old residents did not want to mend their ways and co-operate with the spring cleaning. I felt we had marvellous scope for public health teaching, but we had to move vary warily. Gradually we made an almost miraculous change in the place. The inmates commented on the increased amount of food since UNRRA took over, so we gather that a large amount had been going elsewhere. They appreciated the cleanliness too.

Today we have clean bedrooms with a babies' nursery where the mothers feed their infants by a fire. There are gay English patchwork quilts on the cots, and calico bags at head and foot for clean and soiled linen, and pretty name cards with pink and blue bows. A hygienic feeding bottle system is available where necessary, although we encourage breast feeding of course.

The mothers now willingly rise before breakfast, which they take in the dining room, instead of lying in bed until midday. The *Kinder bad zimmer* (baby's bathroom) is a gem. We were fortunate in finding ten wooden tables of uniform size. These, covered with sheets, are arranged so that the mothers move in rotation, undressing the baby on one, soaping on the next, bathing and drying further on, and lastly dressing again. Above the tables are individual hooks for washers and towels, and in the centre of the room a soiled linen container.

A German Oberschwester, Alexis Strauer, and her friend and assistant Schwester Aniliese Otte, both experienced in infant care, really have been responsible for the success of the place. I gave them everything I could find, told them what I wanted, and they and the mothers made baby clothing, towels, etc., marking all with 'UNRRA' in pink and blue thread, which the Germans mysteriously produced. They supervise the bathing and seventeen babies are washed and dressed in forty minutes. The mothers are so happy they do not want to move back to the Camp when the time comes!

We have thirty-five beds and cots in this Home now and thirty-eight Maternity beds in the Glyn Hughes Hospital, so keep a steady flow moving from one to the other. And so ended my drive round the camp that day.

Hohne
28th November 1945

There was great excitement among the staff and patients today. The results of the Luneberg trials have just reached us. Thirty out of the forty-five were sentenced. Eleven are to hang, including Kramer, Dr Klein, Irma Grese, Juana Bormann and Elizabeth Volkenrath. Nineteen were sentenced to terms of imprisonment varying from life to one year. Kramer was sentenced to death for his part in exterminating at least four million Allied nationals while commandant of the gas chamber at Auschwitz and later Belsen starvation camp.

They say the eleven arch criminals heard the death sentence passed without emotion, but that outside the court Irma Grese burst into violent sobs, Volkenrath wept silently and Bormann appeared to be in a dream. No doubt this was a bit of stage show for their relatives and friends. That ending seems too easy for them somehow, when we think of the untold suffering they have caused.

The UNRRA staff are most interested because every member was able to spend one day at the trials and there has been a good deal of speculation regarding the result.

I have been very distressed over the results of an incident which happened during my trip to London for my Investiture. I was asked by the BBC to broadcast some of my experiences at Belsen and during this broadcast I explained that our hospital now served a population of some 21 000 in the displaced persons camp, and among our patients were a large number suffering from Tb. My story apparently was translated and published in a French newspaper, *Libre*, on 22nd October, last. Alas! The translation read, '. . . that there remained in Belsen 21 000 people ill in hospital', where I was *Nurse in Chief*. This statement brought me a shower of heart-rending letters and photographs from all over France—wives, mothers, sweethearts and friends, all waiting for news of missing relatives and clutching at any straw.

One woman states that her husband was a doctor, forty years old, who with his friend had been committed by the Germans to a concentration camp at Saxenhausen in 1944 and transferred to

Bergen-Belsen in February 1945, liberated on 15th April and admitted to hospital on 2nd May. His friend was fifty-one years old, last seen in March 1945 at Belsen.

Another wrote of her husband, sixty-four years old, who was arrested in Caen by the Gestapo and transferred from Compiègne to Neuengamme camp in Germany, and later to Belsen. She says:

> Miss, I read in the journal *Libres* about the work done for the DPs from Belsen. In this article you give the number of 21 000 ill persons in this camp. Allow me to put the question if all these ill people are French and if yes, if the French authorities have a complete list of those French? I put this question to you because my husband was deported a political prisoner to Bergen-Belsen. He was seen there the last time in January 1945, by a comrade who went on transport at that moment. Since this time I don't know anything about him. He was a strong man but he was then weak as all the men.
>
> My sorrows are ineffable and I always wait for news which never comes. I will be very grateful if you will be so kind to answer my letter and to tell me if the names of those ill persons are known in France and where I have to ask for them. Hoping you will have pity with my sorrow and you will answer soon, I thank you very much for your troubles.

Another, a Madame D asks, 'Good or bad, in any case, I ask you to give me some news and tell me if I can hope still.' She refers to her husband, a postmaster, fifty-six years of age. Her letter reads as follows:

> A mother begs, Miss, allow me to write this letter. Please excuse me for that, but I hope you will understand me. In some words I give you the point in question. I am a mother of six children and during this cursed war I had my two older sons in Germany.
>
> One of them was POW and has come back 1st July, the other one, the younger boy, was deported for work by the Germans and has not yet come back. Where is he? I don't know. I can tell you that, after the news I got, he has suffered very much since December 1944, or January 1945, when he was put in a concentration camp near Hamburg and at least I got an *avis de repatriement* from Camp Sandbostel between Bremen and Hamburg. His brother saw him in the bed at the hospital in Sandbostel at the end of June. One has emptied the camp and

> since then I don't know where he is. Miss, think about my grief, he has been liberated by the British and I hope, too, you can give some news about my dear little child.

She goes on to say she heard my broadcast and then continues, 'Miss, you who see so much suffering think please about the sorrows of a mother who does not know anything about her dear little son.' She gives me her son's name and says he was born in 1923, and was deported by the Germans as a slave worker in Hamburg and then to a prison in Luneberg, and after that to a concentration camp from which he was liberated on 7th May 1945. She concludes, 'I implore you, Miss, give me an answer and tell me if you will be so kind to make enquiries in other hospitals.'

Day after day these letters came. Irma translated them all. I sent them to the BRCS officials at the camp-tracing bureau. The tragedy is that these missing people might have been among the thousands who perished here without leaving a trace as to their identity.

The error in the translation of my broadcast with the BBC had caused these wounds to be re-opened and I regret it more than I can say.

I was horrified at first thinking that I might have made a misleading statement and could hardly wait after receiving the first letter to re-read my scripts and re-assure myself that I had been accurate. A personal letter was sent to every enquiry but unfortunately without any hope.

You remember the list of deficiencies we had to supply in July last—well, we've never heard another word, nor have the deficiencies been made up! My latest worry is cups. We have over 400 patients today and 223 cups and so we are forced to use empty jam tins. As we have no sterilisers, all our china in the Tb wards has to be soaked in disinfectant after use, and this prevents us from using these cups in other wards. A constant SOS has been issued but to date one would think there were no cups in Germany. How I would like to be able to poke round in some of the German cellars!

We heard the siren wailing two or three times today and found that it is being used to warn of a DP raid on one of the German farms round here.

This is an amazing place. The other day the German Matron came to me to request the transfer of three of her nurses because

October24th. 1945

To Miss Muriel DOHERTY,
Nurse in Chief of the U.N.R.R.A.

B E L S E N Camp.

Madam,

Having read in a French Nespaper called "LIBRE" of October 22nd. last that there remained In BELSEN 21.000 people ill in Hospital where you are Nurse in Chief, I take the liberty of writing to you to ask you if you would be able to obtain some information regar_ -ding my husband, Political Convict, in this Camp and a friend of his.

Enclosed please find an information bill & a photo.

With all my thanks for what you can do for me, I remain, Madam,

Yours faithfully,

Jenny Delmas

Correspondence from J. Deimas-Marsalet to Muriel Doherty, Belsen, 1945

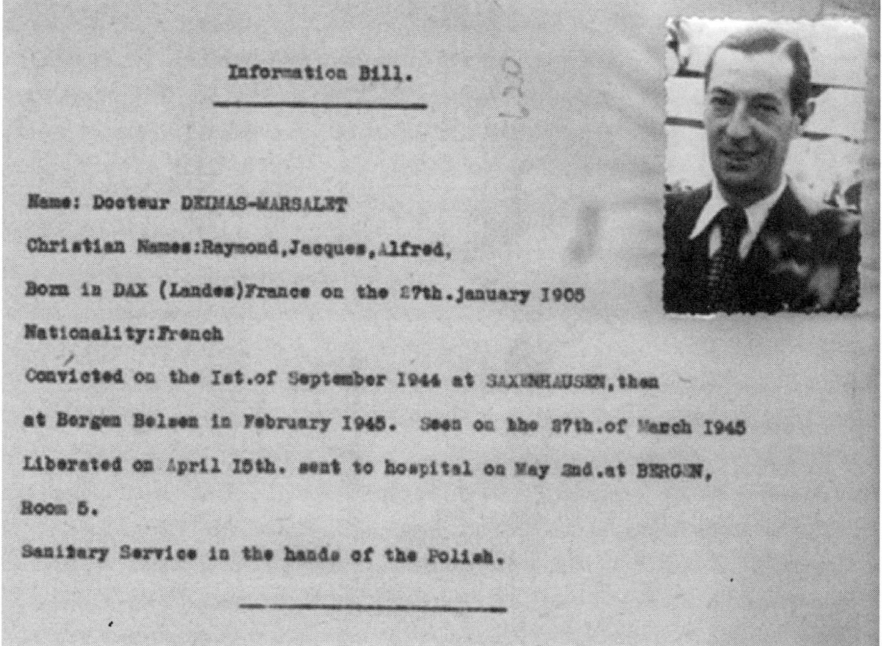

Information Bill.

Name: Docteur DEIMAS-MARSALET

Christian Names:Raymond,Jacques,Alfred,

Born in DAX (Landes)France on the 27th.january 1905

Nationality:French

Convicted on the Ist.of September 1944 at SAXENHAUSEN,then

at Bergen Belsen in February 1945. Seen on hhe 27th.of March 1945

Liberated on April 15th. sent to hospital on May 2nd.at BERGEN,

Room 5.

Sanitary Service in the hands of the Polish.

Information bill contained in correspondence from J. Deimas-Marsalet to Muriel Doherty, Belsen, 1945

they were disturbing the staff. 'Why?' I enquired. 'Because they are communists,' she replied. Now, what a problem! How can I, being British and therefore an ally (whether I like it or not) of the Soviets, agree with the ex-enemy German Matron on something I know is quite probably true? Without appearing to show my sympathy towards the German Matron, I listened and made the mental reservation that I would remove the said nurses when our next exchange takes place.

Such is life! It sometimes requires the utmost diplomacy to avoid becoming embroiled in the seething whirlpool of politics, which looks as if it would engulf Europe.

The new reduced British Army Ration Scale for Displaced Persons in Hospital came into use on 1st November. There was a great amount of dissatisfaction among the patients, who felt they should be given more. There is less variety and the meat ration has been cut, but the caloric value has been maintained at 2316 per day by the addition of other items, and we try to give the Tb patients as much extra nourishment as possible.

Unfortunately raw milk is not always available now in the necessary quantity and eggs are very scarce—in fact we have not had any in hospital for six weeks. We have almost used the last of our rolled oats from the Red Cross parcels and apparently there is to be no more issued from Army sources.

The cut in bread from sixteen to twelve ounces per person per day is another point of dissension and the men frequently request an extra slice of bread, which it is not always possible to give. Added to this, we know the German staff are pilfering a great deal of the patients' food and we are doing our best to prevent this. The other day the men in the A2 (Surgical) Ward demanded to know why those in A3 (Tb) had bread, butter, cheese and milk at 3 pm and they had not!

Food is still the most important thing in the lives of these people. All the male patients were out of bed in Ward B today, angry at the cut in the bread ration. They told me that they read in the papers that in Brazil, Canada and the USA the ration was not cut, and demanded the Red Cross parcels which the papers stated were coming to Belsen—and which they had not received. Actually, these parcels were insufficient to give to individual patients and so were added to the general ration for all and issued accordingly.

I found our Welfare Officer and asked her to explain the position and to write a bulletin for all wards giving an account of the food situation in the world, and particularly the UK and Europe today.

As soon as the facts were explained and they were convinced we were not putting one over, these men were satisfied that they were getting a fair deal and were ready to co-operate. I have found that ignorance of the facts and misunderstanding is the cause of trouble in most cases.

The laundry problem is so acute at present that I decided to go and see for myself why we were not receiving the stuff we sent up. The British QM, who by the way is a Jew from South Africa and very sympathetic towards our problems, took me to the laundry and at a glance we saw why we were losing so much. Men and women from the camp were coming and going as they liked with bundles of linen under their arms. Hungarian soldiers were doing the same. DP girls, employed in the laundry were lounging about knitting and chewing. No one in charge could be found at first, but we finally came upon a British Sergeant and the Captain made his wishes known in no uncertain terms. All doors are to be kept locked except one entrance, and two days weekly are to be set aside entirely for hospital work.

Great excitement on 16th November; the camp was closed after reveille at 4 am. Four battalions of British troops were brought in and a room-to-room search carried out for firearms, alcohol, black-market goods, etc. As we drove from our mess to the hospital that morning, Bren guns covered us at every turning—the place was just bristling. I believe they found masses of stuff, including a horse ready for slaughter in an upstairs room!

One day recently, 18th November, nine ambulances arrived and disgorged some fifty patients and a group of females at the hospital gates. They were Russian POW Tb patients in transit, of whose expected arrival we had been notified some hours before.

I saw a commotion near Reception and walked over to enquire. The interpreter told me that there were four Russian nurses, two doctors and several orderlies who intimated that they wished to inspect the hospital accommodation and preparations before they would allow their patients to enter!

I asked the interpreter to bring the nurses to me, which he did. They bounced up, heads thrown defiantly back, and planting their feet apart and arms akimbo, glared at me. I decided this was a time when I became a firm but tactful British Matron, so I addressed the one in charge, who turned her back, muttered something and walked away. I was then determined her manner would change, and asked my interpreter what she had said. I was told that she refused to speak to a German! They evidently did not know UNRAA was in charge. Apparently they had never heard of that organisation, but after a lengthy explanation they changed their attitude and were quite friendly. Before they left us they pressed some fine US raisins upon me and we had a friendly conversation!

Well, you have no idea of the noise they made—they just took possession. The DPs all hopped out of bed and rushed into the corridors when the news that the Russians had arrived spread. No 'by your leave' or any other courtesy, they just occupied the place, and were halfway through their own rations when our hot meal was served—they were ravenous, poor things.

That evening I went round with one of my nurses, Miss Lazecko, a Canadian of Russian parentage, who herself speaks Russian well. I had a word with every man to make sure they were comfortable—most were rather sullen and looked at us suspiciously, but they were probably very tired after their long journey. However, I did not feel quite happy about them so repeated the tour the next morning, and got into deep water when Miss Lazecko tried to answer their enquiries as to my nationality. She just couldn't get it over—first they thought I was an Austrian, and then, hoping to clarify things, she explained that I was Australian, one of those Australians who has fought the Japs. I suppose it was the first time these illiterate peasant soldiers had ever heard of Australia, for they immediately jumped frigidly to the conclusion that I was a Jap!

Finally light appeared to dawn on one more intelligent-looking man, who explained the confusion, and they laughed at their mistake and we passed on to the next bed.

I had told the German Matron that they were expected and that I required her staff to prepare rooms for the Russian staff as well as wards for the patients. It was funny to see the German nurses spring to it. They openly admitted that they were terrified of the Russians and were extremely anxious to have everything in readiness, in their typically servile way when force is concerned. They stood about in groups whispering when the Russians actually arrived—German and Hungarian orderlies sprang to it and hastened to carry baggage or push stretchers. It really was funny to watch.

As they were being taken to their wards they passed one or two Polish wards and must have noticed sheets and pillow cases on the beds. Anyway, that evening they demanded sheets because the Poles had them, but we had no sheets or pillow cases and this called for appeasement, for we were in the throes of one of our frequent breakdowns in the laundry owing to shortage of coal and had received no fresh linen for over a week. The situation was not improved when we asked them to sign for the blankets and towels we lent them!

A convoy of ambulances came to take them to the train after lunch the next day, and we all heaved a sigh of relief as we saw them depart. However, shortly afterwards they all returned as the train had to have two wheels changed. So we unloaded, and loaded again. Fortunately the electricity was on and we gave them a hot meal at fifteen minutes' notice at 4.30 pm, and they finally left at 7 pm and we don't know if we have all our blankets or not, because the Jerrys can't count and we've not had time.

In spite of everything I think they all departed feeling more or less satisfied, and perhaps more enlightened than when they arrived.

On 11th November we were invited to Gimlet Sunday at the 4th Wilts' Officers' Mess—the Gimlet is a mixture of gin, bitters and cucumber—but the refrigerator in the basement interested me far more. As you will remember, I had been told that Kramer, the Beast of Belsen, had spent many uneasy hours within its portals when the British caught him. I do not know whether they were so busy and so few that, not knowing what to do with him, just popped him in for a while! Or whether he popped himself in when he saw the British coming!

When Miss Delaney was doing rounds in Hospital one evening recently she found the patients from the Tb and surgical wards milling round something in the corridor and gaily laughing and rollicking about in a precarious manner. On closer investigation she saw a large barrel, which by this time was nearly empty, and the patients we suspect were very full. Anyway, she was invited to join the party and sample the alcoholic beverage, which probably resulted from a raid on a German potato crop. I am sure the mere fact that they were able to have a bit of sly grog did them all a great deal of good, and there were no ill effects and the donor remains unknown.

Talking of crops, I went to Hanover to see my sick nurse recently. It was a lovely sunny day and we ate our lunch by the roadside. Everywhere the Germans were busily putting turnips in huge mounds with straw and earth, for the winter. This was in contrast to the apparent apathy in clearing up the damaged areas—their attitude appears to be that the Allies caused much of it so they can clear it up.

We have been having an awful time again with the linen room—thought my new system was fine until I found the German blacksmith, boilerman, orderlies and cleaning women were all being issued with clean linen by the Russian girl in charge! Followed a week or so making the system water-tight again.

America has just announced that she is making her contribution to UNRRA for another year, so all is well. It would be too awful if our help to these unfortunate people in Europe and elsewhere should cease just now.

I remember how my late DGMS solemnly asked me if I was sure I was safely tied up financially with UNRRA before he would agree to release me from the RAAFNS. He certainly had foresight or premonition!

A train load of about 2300 Poles arrived recently at Bergen-Belsen railway station and refused to alight as they would not come to the same place as the Poles from the Concentration Camp! It transpires that they and their families had been volunteer workers for the Germans.

The British troops were angry when they were called out next day to disentrain them. Several fire engines were taken down and the hoses made ready; 3 pm was zero hour and not one was moving from the train. We heard that the hoses were used, and at 9 pm the troops were still driving lorry loads of these people into the Camp. As their Sunday rest day had been spoiled, we suspect they took their time and dumped them at the Camp gates to find their own way to HQ. I think I would have made them walk all the way.

It is very difficult to see why these volunteers should be given free board and lodging and all the perks the genuine DPs have here. Most of them were well dressed and looked fairly well fed, but of course we cannot discriminate. When we think of Britain giving up so much to feed the starving in Europe and we see who sometimes receives the food, it makes us furious. On the other hand, attractive enticements were offered by the Germans to these foreign volunteers and those who accepted could only have known what the Nazis told them and we all know how powerful their propaganda was. That is just another of the many problems that must be solved before we win the peace.

We had a great stir recently when we thought we saw Adolf Hitler in the guise of one of the German gardeners here. We spoke of this likeness for several days and then, hearing that the Führer was supposed to have been seen in Hamburg recently, we were all agog. He is the image, in faded uniform and moustache complete.

It became too much for my inquisitive nature and I took a close walk round and admired the smart 'UNRRA' he was composing of red and white pebbles in the lawn at the entrance. Unless he'd been injected with the stuff some of the South Sea Islanders use for shrinking skulls, I'm afraid I can't claim the reward, and although it *was* like him in the distance I could not bring myself to greet him as Adolf!

The German nurses still try all sorts of dodges to get leave to travel to Hamburg. One day a telegram arrived on a German form from some distracted relative recalling a nurse, and before I had time to do anything another one came. They were just too smart, but by that time I had enquired and found that it was not possible to send telegrams in Germany—they have only just now got some sort of a postal service in action! Compassionate leave is not granted without a medical certificate, but unfortunately the German doctors are ever ready to oblige their compatriots, which makes it rather difficult at times.

Continued 26th November 1945

The mothers invited me to an exhibition of their work yesterday. They had made some attractive sets of baby clothes, all beautifully embroidered to their own designs, out of some of those rather useless canary-coloured wraps which our QM had found in his wanderings.

There were also samples of their cake and biscuit making, which we were invited to taste with a cup of coffee. Krysstow was, of course, well to the fore and his mother beamed proudly when I nursed him. This meant, however, that I had to nurse every other baby in the home so that no one would be upset. It was such a happy party.

A heavy fall of soft feathery snow two days ago has transformed the whole place from bare bleakness to fairyland. The symmetry of the firs was enhanced by the snow, which covered everything. I've never seen anything so lovely and I felt elated. The evenings are even more beautiful than the days, with the shimmering lights among the whiteness. The snowfall has ceased now and the thaw has set in, causing frozen and dangerously glassy roads and paths.

Official guests at a ceremony representing organisations at Belsen, 1945. Muriel Doherty sits at the end of the third row, nearest the camera.

Hohne
6th December 1945

I was invited to the Belsen Jewish School, Beth Sefer Ivri, Chanukkah concert yesterday at 5 pm in the large tented theatre, where there was a packed and appreciative audience. It was all rather tragic, but very well presented.

The ceremony of lighting the Chanukkah candles was interesting, and the singing of the choir sweet. The Junior class did a pretty dance of the candles and a young girl, Lola Kuschenblatt, the Dance of Liberation. The choir concluded the concert singing 'Hatikvah', the Jewish National Anthem.

It is amazing how cleverly they made the costumes out of practically nothing. *The Miracle*, in which the first scene was on the Shores of Tel Aviv and the second a children's colony a year later, was particularly well done. Oh! If only there were some solution to the problems of these unfortunate Jewish people, some part of the world which they could call their own, just as every other race does. They might find some relief from their mental sufferings and live without fear of further persecution. We have seen and heard so much of their sorrows here at Belsen, and it seems terrible that these children of an oppressed race should not have the security and freedom for which our men fought and died.

Later: 14th December

Last Sunday, 12th December, Dr Tewsley and I were invited to a circumcision ceremony, to be performed on the first Jewish boy to be born in the Glyn Hughes Hospital and the first in the camp since liberation. You can imagine how great was the excitement everywhere.

The sitting room in RB 5, our Mothers' Convalescent Home, was specially decorated and a long table in one corner, covered with a sheet, held scalpel, spirits and surgical dressings, whilst a freshly made cot stood nearby. The Chief Welfare Officers of the Jewish Welfare Committee, the Rabbi (an Englishman), twelve Polish men friends, six women, and the professional circumcisionist completed the party. On arrival, Dr Tewsley and I were introduced all round, which included the courteous kissing of hands which is so charming.

It was a tremendous event for the operator, who, although he had actually performed over 700 before the war, was obviously nervous. Under the Nazi regime, performing the rite of circumcision was an offence, punishable by death, and as all Jewish babies born in the Concentration Camps were destroyed, he had not had any practice for some considerable time. It was such an interesting ceremony that I shall describe the procedure as I saw it from the aseptic point of view, without meaning to belittle its importance in any way. We thought we had prepared everything they would require to make it a success, but just as the operation was about to begin we found the father was missing! We finally ran him to earth in the Maternity wing of the Glyn Hughes where the mother was in bed suffering from a paralytic ileus. Apparently the reason for the father's late arrival was that he and his wife could not decide on the child's name! They told me that the Jewish son is always called after a deceased member, usually the mother's father or grandfather. As there was no trace of her father since he was sent to a concentration camp, they had to decide on some other deceased.

While this was going on, the star performer donned a gown and a black skull cap and fidgeted with the wool and bandages on the table, punctuated by wiping his sweating brow on the back of his hand; producing a grubby bit of rag from his pocket and blowing his nose; pouring methylated spirits on his hand, tasting it and then proceeding to rub the remainder on the cut up bits of wool and gauze which he finally arranged on a plate borrowed from the banqueting table. At this time, one of the friends commenced sharpening a wooden-handled, square-bladed knife on an oilstone, produced from a velvet bag. Another heavily bearded man was rocking backwards and forwards in a corner, audibly praying. The knife blade was tried first on the finger nails and then on the palm of the sharpener's hand, and we were becoming very concerned lest some infection be conveyed to the child.

A plate of earth having been added to the table equipment, the operator dangled a length of bandage on the floor, wiped his forehead with it, patted each piece of wool and gauze again, put on a black velour hat over his skull cap and tied the child's knees together. They then began incantations, while the crying infant, nestling on a pillow, was handed from one to the other of the six men, one of whom sat on a chair with a stool at his feet, donned a *tamplit* and held the infant for the operation. After a perfunctory rinsing of hands in a basin of disinfectant and drying them on a towel which had fallen on the floor, the knife was finally tested on the operator's hand and the actual operation performed swiftly, in one movement, with such skill as I have ever seen in any operating theatre. The child was returned to the cot and the heavily laden plates of food were handed round. We were given a glass of neat whisky each, but I quietly and—I hope—unobtrusively placed mine behind the dressings on the table before leaving. You know how I dislike that beverage!

On returning to the Hospital after this very happy party, we found the mother had walked from her ward at the far end of the Hospital to the main door in search of a transport which would convey her to the ceremony! Fortunately she was intercepted and taken back to bed. The endurance of these people is amazing. She had escaped from Poland and hitch-hiked with her husband by irregular borders to Belsen in the ninth month, and had been out chopping wood in the forest the day the baby was born! I was terribly sorry for the operator's nervousness, very pleased that the German nurses had to prepare the things, and most interested in this religious ceremony which was so important to these oppressed and persecuted people. It is to be hoped that they will forever be allowed to settle in a country they can call their own, free to live their own lives without fear, and able to take their own place in world affairs. Then, and then only, can we say that the sacrifices made by our own men and women in World War II were not in vain.

The mother is improving steadily (the walk probably did her good), the babe has not turned a hair, and Jewish history was made at Belsen that day.

It is perishing today—the temperature is 12°C below zero, according to the thermometer outside our mess window. All lights in the hospital went off suddenly at 7 pm this evening—there was chaos in the wards when the patients and visitors became excited and began wandering round in the pitch dark. I tried the call lights over the doors and found they worked, so told the German nurses to switch them on. Alas! They worked from a battery which was soon exhausted and all was inky darkness again.

We had a few tiny wax night lights—flat saucers of cardboard with a layer of tallow and a minute wick in the centre. These, without ten precious lanterns which the German nurses were slow to light, enabled us to see where the patients were and persuade them to go back to bed in this vast and sprawling hospital. Funny, how one never feels nervous in these emergencies. I suppose because one knows that everyone relies on a leader to take the initiative and deal with the situation, whatever it may be.

All the Germans here have been screened by the authorities. They each had to fill in a searching form or *fragenbogen*, which in many cases revealed their activities under the Nazi regime. My senior Oberschwester, Bartels, who joined the Nazi party in 1933, and her sister also an active member, were removed some weeks ago and we are told will lose profession and citizenship. They are both good nurses and speak English well. We have lost a number like this and I always feel they were probably earmarked and trained to take charge of our larger hospitals when the Nazis conquered Britain.

This is a place of contradictions alright! I found a wreath of spruce with four candles on my office table last Sunday week, a German custom; on the first Sunday in Advent they light one candle, on the second, two, and so on. The German Nurses made it for me and they also had them suspended from various lights in the Hospital, and have asked if they may sing carols at Christmas—it's all so contradictory as they frequently neglect the DPs and pilfer their food on a large scale. I have two languishing in jail at present, awaiting enquiry.

My UNRRA staff are still truly sensational—English, Scottish, Australian, Canadian, Belgian, French, Dutch, Danish and Eire, and I have just lost my last American nurse, Miss Szloch, who has taken up her original assignment in Poland, which was delayed owing to the Polish Government's tardiness in inviting UNRRA to their country.

You will ask how I have managed with the language problem here. Well, the UNRRA staff all speak English and so with a dash of German, some bad French, a smattering of Polish, I manage to understand and make myself understood to the patients, all of whom speak at least one other language as well as their own. I also have my interpreter-secretary when things become too complicated!

It is amusing at meals sometimes, but we are a very happy staff and only wish we had more time to exchange ideas on nursing matters in our respective countries. It has been a wonderful experience for me to see and hear the strong and weak points of the training in the various countries and to appreciate what is lacking in our own and where we can strengthen it—for strengthen it we must if we are to hold our own with the nursing profession of the world.

My staff has a fair amount of recreational facilities here now—horse-riding, walking, dancing at the Officers' Club, hockey and football matches to attend, cinema and frequent concerts both here and in nearby towns. With large British Army and Air Force Units all round we do not lack amusement, which is so very necessary when doing work of this kind.

I saw some enterprising DP lads and lassies skating on the very thin ice on Swan Lake yesterday! Am quite accustomed to the cold and love the snow—really feel better in this bracing air than the humid weather of New South Wales, but do wish someone would invent an anti-blush substance for one's nose!

We now have only one German *Sanitator* (orderly) in the hospital, instead of ten or twelve—they are being demobilised, and as fast as this happens they abscond and we don't see them again!

This will probably be my last community letter from Belsen—I have been offered the position with UNRRA of Chief Nurse for Poland and have decided to accept—Belsen is on its feet, the Hospital is organised as far as possible, and it is only a matter of carrying on for the winter, as we hope the DPs will be settled somewhere after that, either in their own country or elsewhere. That is a problem we fortunately do not have to solve here but we actually can see no solution for the stateless people, which worries us very much. There are 7000 Jews here at present, all victims of Nazi terror. We also have twelve 'pure Aryans' in Hospital and we are feeling very annoyed that our new SMO should have admitted them. Pilfering by the Germans is gaining alarming proportions—doctors, nurses and cleaners—are stealing masses of food meant for our patients. I found one of the German doctors' wives wending her way along the cellar corridor to the kitchen the other day. Under her arm she had a large basin of little red berries which grow wild here. I allowed her to reach the kitchen, where she was issued with a large quantity of precious sugar by one of her compatriots, and then asked the QM to deal with the matter officially. We frequently unearth masses of food hidden in the ward linen cupboards, and various other places. The German Oberschwester holds the keys of these utility cupboards—with such a small UNRRA staff it is quite impossible to arrange otherwise and constant supervision is well nigh impossible.

My new job sounds interesting and I have been told that my duties will include advising the Polish Ministry of Health on all problems of nursing organisation, administration and training, and to be concerned with the training of public health nurses at the National Institute of Hygiene. I hear there are only about twenty-two million people left in Poland, out of about thirty-five million in 1939. In a way the whole invitation is humorous for, as you know, I, with others, have been trying for about eight years in my own country to awaken those responsible to the need for re-organisation and now a foreign country invites me to advise them! It sounds as if it would be a construction rather than re-construction, after all their country has suffered, and I am looking forward to it very much.

Our preparations for Christmas here are well under way, and already a shining star sends its joyful message from a specially planted fir tree on the Hospital lawn. It will be interesting to see the Poles in their own country and not as DPs and will be a relief to get away from the Germans. My HQ will be Warsaw, but until I report to HQ European Regional Office, London, in the very near future, I shall not know any details. By the way, Kramer and ten of his men and women SS guards were hanged in Hameln, a hundred miles south of Hamburg, on 13th December. Volkenrath, Grese and Bormann were the first to die—Kramer, Grese and five others had appealed against their sentences but General Montgomery, as Commander of the British Zone, had turned them down.

I shall be very sorry to leave Belsen and all my contacts here as it has been the greatest experience of my life, and with all its trials and tribulations I have loved every moment of it. In undertaking this relief work of helping others to help themselves we knew

Muriel Doherty (standing, right) in Cracow, Poland, 1946

no assignment would be permanent, so that I feel, having done my best for Belsen, I can make a definite contribution to the Health Services in Poland. I do not know anything about my staff yet except that Miss Szloch will be with me, for which I am very pleased.

You may find my style is cramped in letter writing from Poland as I understand there is strict censorship under the Red control. However, do keep on writing, you have no idea what a joy it is to see the mail arriving.

Appendix I

'BELSEN LIBERATION ANNIVERSARY MARKED BY CEREMONIES'

Extract from UNRRA European Regional Office, 4 May 1946

The anniversary of the liberation of Belsen was recently marked by special ceremonies at the barracks where today 18 000 displaced persons are living under the care of UNRRA. April 15 1945 saw British mobile columns roll up to the walls of the notorious concentration camp, and set free the living remains of once healthy human beings. Today the old camp is levelled to the ground and completely ploughed under; the old buildings have been replaced by mass graves and the site is now usually deserted. The comfortable barracks which today house the displaced persons are some distance away. This assembly centre was first organised by British Army authorities shortly after the liberation of the concentration camp; the UNRRA assumed responsibility for the centre's administration late in February.

The Poles in their new camp, who number almost 9000, many of whom are awaiting repatriation, observed the occasion with a quiet church service followed by festivities. But for the 9000 members of the Jewish camp, the event, falling as it did on the eve of the traditional Passover festival, was a much more sombre one. In a special ceremony attended by visiting British Army and Military Government officers and personnel from UNRAA, and some half dozen cooperating volunteers and agencies, the Jewish DPs unveiled a monument commemorating the 30 000 Jews who had been slaughtered at Belsen. Standing on the site of the old camp, the granite and marble stone base [of the monument bore an] inscription, chiselled in English and Hebrew, [which read] 'Israel and the world shall remember 30 000 Jews exterminated in the concentration camps of Bergen-Belsen, at the hand of the murderous Nazis. Earth conceal not the blood shed on the first anniversary of liberation April 15.' Speaking in English after the unveiling, one of the camp leaders said they stood on the spot that was a stigma for all Germany. Declaring that many of his people could have been saved had the statesmen of the world proved more human and less compromising during the pre-war years, he added, 'Every concession resulted in the death of hundreds of thousands of Jews. Now we stand here and bow our heads in memory of six million dead.'

Earlier a parade stretching several miles in length had taken the thousands of Jews from their own camps to the scene of the ceremony. Almost all of them between the ages of fifteen and thirty-five, they marched now as a healthy-looking group, holding aloft their banners and flags.

Arriving at the site of the memorial, the parade disbanded and the gathering unveiled the monument, with traditional Jewish commemoration services. The stone itself was used as a pulpit and the assembled Jewish displaced persons prayed fervently.

On all sides of the thousands who witnessed yesterday's ceremony lay the massed graves, marked and levelled out like innocuous garden plots. Pieces of charred clothing could still be found, as could some human bones, and the chimney of the incinerator still stood ominously in the distant corner of the field.

Present were Colonel Agnew of the British Red Cross Society, Brigadier Stawell, UNRRA Deputy Chief of Operations in Germany, and Major-General Fanshawe, Deputy Director of UNRRA in the British Zone.

Several hundred of the 18 000 displaced persons at the nearby UNRRA assembly centre had been original inmates of the same concentration camp. The majority, however, had come from the entire countryside, and in many cases been in other concentration camps in Germany. The 9000 Jews contributed almost the entire number of Jewish DPs in the British Zone of Germany.

Doherty Collection, Yad Vashem Archives, Jerusalem, Israel, 0–70/36, volume 3, pp. 365–6.

Appendix II

MURIEL KNOX DOHERTY: A BIOGRAPHICAL NOTE

An article appearing in a London newspaper described Muriel Knox Doherty as 'a practical-looking woman, with a kindly smile, [who] had one rule only in her Belsen hospital. It was "No rules and regulations allowed". She ran her hospital for the maimed in body and soul without orders.'

Miss Doherty was an outstanding Australian nurse who made many contributions to the profession throughout her long and varied career. She was, for example, an exceptional clinical nurse, a well-loved nurse teacher, and a skilled nurse administrator. Always willing to try something new, to take up a challenge, she remained passionate throughout her long life about her beloved nursing and did whatever she could to advance the profession.

At the same time she was an avid collector of material about nursing and anything that related to nursing and the health-care sector. She was a hoarder of memorabilia about her own life as well, and it would appear that she very rarely threw anything away.

Miss Doherty, unlike many nurses of her generation, wrote long letters about the people she met and what she thought of them; events in her own life; letters to newspapers, politicians and government bodies, and anyone she thought might be able to help her achieve something that she saw as necessary for nursing. Once she had decided that something needed to be done, she single-mindedly pursued her vision until it became a reality.

As well as writing about everything, she also kept copies of almost everything she wrote, and much of this collection is now held in the Doherty Collection at the New South Wales College of Nursing, where it remains a largely unmined source on nursing, Miss Doherty herself, and the health-care sector in general. Other parts of her collection appear in a variety of places throughout Australia and overseas, including the Mitchell Library (Sydney), the National Library (Canberra), the Archives at the National War Memorial (Canberra), and the Yad Vashem Archives in the Holocaust Museum, Jerusalem, Israel. She also left behind three manuscripts, two of which have already been published. The first is a very detailed history of the Royal Prince Alfred Hospital, her beloved training school.[1] The second is her autobiography, which gives many insights into her professional life.[2] The third manuscript contained the letters written to her family and friends during her time as Matron of the Bergen-Belsen concentration Camp, and form the basis of this book.

Miss Doherty began her nurse training at the Royal Prince Alfred Hospital in Sydney, on 5 November 1921. Prior to this she was a teacher in a private girls' school for three years, and resigned during World War I, at the age of twenty-one, to take up full-time voluntary Red Cross work. She joined the Australian Red Cross Number 6 Voluntary Aide Detachment at North Sydney, gaining her St John's Ambulance First Aid and Home Nursing Certificate, and continued this voluntary work whilst helping out at home until 1921.

Early in 1919 the worldwide pneumonic influenza epidemic hit Sydney, decimating the population. Miss Doherty went to work at the Royal Prince Alfred Hospital, in her capacity as a voluntary aide, to assist with the care of those stricken with this deadly disease. Her work so impressed the then matron, Miss Boissier, that she was asked to consider commencing her nurse training. Due to family reasons Miss Doherty was unable to do this until two years later, in 1921. She loved every bit of her four-year training as a nurse and called this period the happiest years of her life.

Following her graduation as a registered nurse in 1925, at which she was awarded the Alfred Roberts Medal for general proficiency,

---

1 Doherty, M. K. (1996) *The Life and Times of the Royal Prince Alfred Hospital, Sydney, Australia*, edited by R. L. Russell, New South Wales College of Nursing, Sydney.

2 Doherty, M. K. (1996) *Off the Record: The Life and Times of Muriel Knox Doherty 1896–1988*, edited by R. L. Russell, New South Wales College of Nursing, Sydney.

The changing face of Muriel Knox Doherty. Clockwise, from top left: as a student nurse at Royal Prince Alfred Hospital, Sydney (c. 1921); her passport photograph in 1954; and as a most active senior citizen (c. 1975)

Miss Doherty took up an appointment as a Charge Nurse in the gynacology ward at the Royal Prince Alfred, and was promoted to Sister-in-Charge after six months.

Early in 1930 she decided she wanted to go to England. She had managed to save £100, a not insubstantial sum given the poor salary of nurses at this time. It was enough for a one-way fare to London. She was thrilled to be in England, and her records demonstrate how strong her patriotic and personal feelings for the old country were.

She then took the important personal decision to enter the Sister Tutor course at King's College of Household and Social Sciences, University of London. At the time there was no similar course available in Australia and there was only one qualified nurse teacher in New South Wales. Miss Doherty's main motivation for undertaking this course was her desire to contribute to improving nursing in Australia.

Having successfully completed the Sister Tutor course, she returned to the Royal Prince Alfred, where she was responsible for establishing a model nurse training school, and for introducing the first preliminary training school in New South Wales. The model nurse training school catered for nursing students across the four years of the general nursing program and was preceded by the preliminary training school, an innovation within New South Wales. Nursing students attended the preliminary training school, receiving both theoretical and clinical tuition, for a number of weeks prior to commencing their training and entering the wards on a full-time basis. Prior to the establishment of this school, nursing students commenced working in the wards without receiving any tuition. In her first year as Sister Tutor, Miss Doherty was responsible for 230 nursing students, and her average workload was sixty-five hours per week.

Ominous signs of a further world conflict prompted Miss Doherty to respond to an appeal in August 1935 for volunteers for the Australian Army Nursing Service. She was accepted and appointed as a staff nurse in the Army Reserve. In 1939, with the outbreak of World War II, she was called up as Sister Clerk to the Office of the Principal Matron, Miss E. Kearey, Australian Army Nursing Service. But what she really wanted was to go on active service as a nurse (preferably overseas, into the war zone), rather than spending her time in an administrative capacity. She continued to work towards this and was finally offered the choice of a position as Matron of the 1400-bed hospital which was in the process of being built at Concord, in Sydney (and which was to become the Concord General Repatriation Hospital), or Matron in the inaugural Royal Australian Air Force Nursing Service. She chose the latter and in 1940 took up her position as 1st Squadron Leader, Matron-in-Charge, Number 3 RAAF Hospital, Richmond.

Miss Doherty went on to serve with distinction, becoming Principal Matron and gaining a promotion to Wing Commander. Her military services were further recognised in 1945 when she was awarded the Royal Red Cross Medal (1st Class) whilst working in Bergen-Belsen (Germany). Her investiture ceremony, conducted by King George VI at Buckinghamn Palace, London on 16 October 1945, was held exactly six years after her first appointment to the AANS.

At the same time as she was establishing the RAAF Nursing Service, she played a role in the first government committee to investigate nursing in New South Wales. This committee, established by the Minister for Health, published a report with a number of far-reaching recommendations for the reorganisation of the nursing profession in that state. Miss Doherty's files, notes, newspaper clippings, and other documents relating to her work on this committee are held in the State Archives of New South Wales.

In 1944 Miss Doherty co-authored with two other Australian nurse educators the textbook *Modern Practical Nursing Procedures*.[3] This book, which was reprinted many times, was to become the standard introductory textbook for nursing students for many years throughout Australia.

Despite these successes, Miss Doherty still wanted to work overseas, directly in the war zone. To this end she retired from the RAAF Nursing Service in 1945 and joined the United Nations Relief and Rehabilitation Administration organisation, travelling to London before taking up her appointment as the Chief Nurse and Principal Matron of the recently liberated Bergen-Belsen Concentration

3 Doherty, M. K., Sirl, M. B. & Ring, O. I. (1944) *Modern Practical Nursing Procedures*, Dymocks Book Arcade Ltd, Sydney.

Camp. During her busy year at the camp she continued her life-long habit of writing about her experiences and collecting memorabilia.

From Bergen-Belsen she took up a position, through UNRRA, as a consultant to a group working to assist in the rehabilitation of nursing education in Poland. At the end of 1946 Miss Doherty returned to Australia and worked for the establishment of a college of nursing. She went on to become a foundation member of the Council of the New South Wales College of Nursing and an active member of the Council of the Australasian Trained Nurses Association, and she helped to inaugurate the National Florence Nightingale Memorial Committee of Australia, becoming one of its first two vice-presidents.

Upon her return to Australia, Miss Doherty deposited her collection from Bergen-Belsen, including a series of her letters home, with the Jewish community in Sydney. The community subsequently asked her permission to send this important and unique collection to the Holocaust Museum and Archives (Yad Vashem), then being established in Jerusalem, Israel. Miss Doherty willingly gave permission, and the majority of her collection is now held in these archives.

Miss Doherty travelled widely in Europe from 1955 to 1957, returning to Australia for a short period, before going to live in England in 1961. She returned home for good in 1965 and took up residence in the Queen Mary Nurses Home at the Royal Prince Alfred Hospital, to enable her to undertake further research for her history of the hospital. She continued her active involvement in matters related to nursing and the health-care sector until her death in 1988.

R. Lynette Russell
Sydney, 1999

Appendix III

A NOTE ON UNRRA

The story of the United Nations Relief and Rehabilitation Administration (UNRRA) is the story of forty-eight nations, victorious in war, who banded together to win another victory in peace—it was with sentiments such as these that Muriel Knox Doherty set out to serve at Bergen-Belsen Concentration Camp and then in Poland.

Australia was one of the forty-four countries which in November 1943 signed the initial agreement to form UNRRA, at a ceremony presided over by President Franklin D. Roosevelt at the White House in Washington. By 1946 there were forty-eight member governments and UNRRA had an international civil service of some 9000 persons recruited from these countries.

The agreement to establish UNRRA '. . . was not a spontaneous or hastily improvised document, belonging to any one nation. It began when the first home was destroyed, when the first people came under enemy occupation, when the first indication of human need became evident; it grew out of many minds seeking ways to relieve suffering . . . to aid in the eventual recovery of a war-torn world.'[1]

All recruits to UNRRA were highly specialised in areas such as supply, transport, health, welfare, industry, agriculture or administrative support for the extensive social welfare programs designed to assist people and countries devastated by war. Miss Doherty's work at Bergen-Belsen was just one of UNRRA's projects to provide health care and assistance to displaced persons and refugees, but it is interesting to note that more than half of the UNRRA

1 UN Information Organisation (1944) *Helping People to Help Themselves: The Story of the United Nations Relief and Rehabilitation Administration*, United Nations, London. p. 3.

personnel were recruited to deal with displaced persons in Germany and Austria.

The original UNRRA agreement stipulated a number of conditions, one of which was that the organisation could not work in any area where the military were operating, without military consent. This explains, in part, many of the administrative difficulties so graphically described by Miss Doherty.

The responsibilities of the Military and UNRAA teams at Belsen, as described in an internal memorandum dated 13 November 1945, were as follows:

UNRRA Responsibilities

A. Command and control of internal teams, including voluntary society teams.
B. Internal administration of assembly centres.
C. Medical, Nursing, Public Health, Dispensary (M.I. Rooms) Hospital aspects, Rehabilitation, Social Welfare, Immunisation.
D. Amenities, including Welfare, Recreation, Education.

Military Responsibilities

A. Overall control, without prejudice to UNRRA responsibilities above.
B. Maintenance of law, order and security in conjunction with Assembly centre direction.
C. Food, fuel, clothing, accommodation (housing and stores), bedding supplies, medical supplies.
D. Until UNRRA's substitute supply of transport, POL, maintenance of vehicles.
E. Supplementary amenity supplies from German sources. The Army will supply suitable office accommodation for the work of UNRRA, and will provide the necessary payment for DPs who are employed. If UNRRA considers that its supply of materials from the Army is inadequate for the maintenance of an efficient service, it can withdraw from its obligations by giving one month's notice. The Army can withdraw from the agreement if the C. in C. is of the opinion that UNRRA is not carrying out its responsibilities in such a way as to cover

him for overall responsibility of DP operations. One month's notice of termination of the Agreement will be given.[2]

By 1946 there were 1 675 000 displaced persons who could not, or did not wish to, be repatriated to their countries of origin. They were considered to be refugees, for whom new homes had to be found. UNRRA was disbanded in December 1946 but its work with displaced persons was continued by such organisations as the International Refugee Organisation, World Health Organization, and the United Nations International Children's Emergency Fund. By early 1952 some one million displaced people had been resettled and a further 73 000 had been successfully repatriated.

Funding for the work of UNRRA was provided by member governments 'whose countries had not been occupied by the enemy'. They contributed roughly one per cent of their national incomes for the year ending 30 June 1943, but the majority of the funding came from the United States of America, the United Kingdom, the British Commonwealth of Nations and the Latin American Republics. Invaded countries that would need relief, such as Russia and China were not assigned quotas.

The work of the UNRRA volunteers is not well documented, which makes Miss Doherty's story an even more important contribution to our knowledge of the events which occurred during and after World War II.

Judith Cornell
Sydney, 1999

2 Doherty Collection, Yad Vashem Archives, Jerusalem, Israel, 0–70/36, volume 4, p. 578.

Appendix IV

FOOD RATION SCALES

35th (Bed) Casualty Clearing Station
Distribution Revised Ration, Belsen Concentration Camp
Issue effective 15th May 1945

Item		Scale 1	Scale 2	Scale 3
1.	Bread, white yeast dough	Nil	10 oz	3½ oz
	or biscuits		7½ oz	
2.	Meat, frozen or fresh	Nil	5 oz	3½ oz
	or boneless	Nil	3¾ oz	2 oz
	or preserved	Nil	3¾ oz	2 oz
3.	Vegetables, fresh	Nil	8 oz	4 oz
	or tinned	Nil	4 oz	2 oz
	or dehydrated	Nil	[?] ½ oz	[?] ¼ oz
4.	Onions, leeks or shallots	Nil	½ oz	½ oz
5.	Potatoes, fresh	Nil	20 oz	4 oz
	Potatoes, dehydrated	Nil	4½ oz	1 oz
6.	Peas or beans or lentils	Nil	1 oz	½ oz
7.	Cheese—skimmed milk	Nil	1 oz	Nil
8.	Sausages (salami or mortadella)	Nil	2½ oz	Nil
9.	Tea	Nil	[not legible]	[not legible]
	or coffee	Nil		
10.	Sugar	1 oz	2 oz	1 oz
11.	Salt	½ oz	½ oz	¼ oz
12.	Jam or syrup or honey	Nil	¼ oz	½ oz
13.	Fruit tinned, sulphated or preserved	Nil	1½ oz	Nil
14.	Milk skimmed, fresh	2 litres	½ litre	1½ litre
	or skimmed, powdered			4½ oz
15.	Pepper	Nil	1/100 oz	Nil
	or paprika	Nil	1/50 oz	Nil
16.	Conc. liquid soup	Nil	Nil	½ oz
17.	Flour	Nil	1 oz	½ oz

Item	Scale 1	Scale 2	Scale 3
18. Oatmeal, spaghetti, macaroni or vermicelli	Nil	Nil	1½ oz
19. Oatmeal		[not legible]	[not legible]
20. Spaghetti, macaroni or vermicelli		[not legible]	[not legible]
21. Fish, tinned (excluding sardines)	Nil	$\frac{4}{9}$ oz	Nil
22. Butter or margarine	Nil	1 oz	1 oz
23. Cooking fat or oil	Nil	$\frac{2}{7}$ oz	Nil
24. Compound vitamin tablets	3 tabs	1 tab	3 tabs

Scale 1: For starvation and serious febrile cases in two hourly feeds
Scale 2: Applies to hospital workers and patients fully convalescent
Scale 3: Applies to hospital patients *not* fully convalescent

Doherty Collection, Yad Vashem Archives, Jerusalem, Israel, 0–70/36, volume 1, item 100A.

Belsen Camp Hospital Ration Distribution Sheet 22 August 1945

Canteen No. Item	Used mostly Scale II		Staff (less a certain amount) Scale III		Total commodities
	Total oz	Patients	Total oz	Patients	
1. Bread (white) yeast, dough	15		5		
or biscuits	7½		3¾		
2. Meat, frozen or fresh	5		3½		
or boneless	3¾		2		
or preserved	3¾		2		
3. Vegetables, fresh	8		4		
4. Onions, leeks or shallots	¾		½		
5. Potatoes, fresh	20		4		
or dehydrated	4¾		1		
6. Peas, beans or lentils	1		½		
7. Cheese, skimmed milk	1		–		
8. Sausage, salami or mortadella	2½		–		
9. Tea or coffee	¼		¼		(if short, some beans baked and ground as substitutes)
10. Sugar	2		1		
11. Salt	¼		¼		
12. Jam, syrup or honey	¾		½		
13. Fruit, tinned, sulphated or preserved	1½		–		
14. Milk, skimmed, fresh	½ litre		1½ litre		Adults skimmed milk. Children full or dried. Maternity full or dried.
15. Pepper	1/100		–		
or paprika	1/50				
16. Conc. soup liquid	–		½		
17. Flour	1		½		
18. Oatmeal, spagetti, macaroni or vermicelli	–		1½		

Canteen No. Item	Used mostly Scale II		Staff (less a certain amount) Scale III		Total commodities
	Total oz	Patients	Total oz	Patients	
19. Oatmeal	1½		–		
20. Spagetti, macaroni or vermicelli	1½		–		
21. Fish—tinned	4/7		–		
22. Butter or margarine	1		1		
23. Cooking fat or oil	2/7		–		
24. Compound vitamin tablets	1		3		

Cigarettes issued when available—two per person per day. German DP staff as well. Eggs and milk to be more severely rationed shortly.

Breakfast 7 am
Dinner 12 midday
Supper 7 pm

Doherty Collection, Yad Vashem Archives, Jerusalem, Israel, 0–70/36, volume 1, item 100B.

Daily scale for DPs/POW, Belsen
In operation 1 November 1945

Commodity	Oz	Grams	Calories
1. Bread (f)	12	336	790
or biscuits (a)	7	196	817
2. Meat, fresh (a)	2	56	114
or meat, tinned (c)	1½	42	102
or meat and vegetables (a)	1½	42	102
3. Vegetables	4	112	17
4. Potatoes	14	392	255
or bread	2	56	132
and flour	¾	21	69
5. Peas or beans or lentils	1	28	85
6. Nutrition food	1	28	94
7. Coffee substitute	½	14	–
or coffee (English)	¾	21	–
8. Sugar	1¼	35	140
9. Milk			
Children (under five years)	½ litre		
or milk, tinned	7	143	46
or milk, powder	2	56	78
Others			
milk, fresh	2	–	–
or milk, tinned	⅔	–	–
or milk, powder	–	–	–
10. Fish—tinned	4/7	16	27
11. Jam	½	14	35
12. Salt	⅜	10½	–
13. Margarine or butter	5/7	20	149
14. Cooking fat or lard	1/7	4	35
15. Soup, dehydrated	½	14	61
or tinned meat	½	14	30
16. Offal or sausage	15/7	48	182
17. Cheese (German)	⅓	10	11
18. Fruit fresh (d)	2	56	18
19. Flour	¾	21	69
TOTAL			2128

Notes: (a) twice a week; (b) once a week; (c) thrice a week; (d) when available; (e) children up to five years of age will get ½ litre of fresh milk or 7 oz tinned milk or 2 oz of milk powder; (f) 10 oz of bread and 1½ oz flour may be drawn in lieu.

Daily Scale C (additional to scales A & B)

Commodity	Grams	Calories
Meat	5	10
Fat	7.5	60
Flour	5	17
Nutrition food	7.5	26
Sugar	8.75	34
Cheese	5	15
Quark (sour milk made into cheese)	5	11
Eggs	5 to 6 per 28 days, when available	
TOTAL		188 [*sic*]

Notes: 1. DPs and POW suffering from Tb will receive the following extra daily rations on the recommendation of the medical officer: 2 eggs, 1.136 litres milk (1¾ pints).
2. Pregnant and nursing mothers, daily after fourth month: ½ litre fresh milk, 100 grams nutritive food.

Daily Extra

Commodity	Grams	Calories
Meat	35	73
Fat	7	53
Bread	143	350
TOTAL		476

Scales A + C combined (adults and children)

Commodity	Oz	Grams	Calories
1. Bread	12	336	790
2. Meat, fresh	2	56 + 5	114 + 60
or tinned	1½	42	102
or meat and vegetables	1½	42	102
3. Vegetables	4	112	17
4. Potatoes	14	392	255
or bread	2	56	132
and flour	¾	21	69
5. Peas or beans or lentils	1	28	85
6. Nutrition Food	1	28 + 7/5	94 + 6
7. Coffee, substitute	½	14	–
Coffee, English	¾	21	–
8. Sugar	1¼	35 + 8.75	140 + 60
9. Milk, fresh	5	0.143 litres	46
Milk, tinned	2	56	78
Milk, powdered	⅔	18	84

Commodity	Oz	Grams	Calories
10. Fish, tinned	4/7	16	27
11. Jam or honey	½	14	35
12. Salt	⅜	10½	–
13. Quark (sour milk made into cheese)	–	5	11
14. Margarine or butter	5/7	20	149
15. Cooking fat or lard	⅕ + 7½	4 + 7	35 + 60
16. Soup, dehydrated or tinned	½	14	61 or 30
17. Offal or sausage	15/7	48	182
18. Cheese (German)	⅓	10 + 5	11 + 15
19. Fruit, fresh	2	56	18
20. Flour	¾	21 + 5	69 + 17
21. Eggs, 5 or 6 per 28 days, when available			

Notes: 1. DPs and POW suffering from Tb will receive the following extra daily rations on the recommendation of the medical officer: 2 eggs, 1.136 litres milk (1¾ pints).
2. Pregnant and nursing mothers should receive daily after the fourth month: ½ litre fresh milk, 100 grams nutrative food

Doherty Collection, Yad Vashem Archives, Jerusalem, Israel, 0–79/36, volume 3, items 334, 336.

Report on Feeding of Patients in Glyn Hughes Hospital, Belsen [Summarised]

Messing Officer,
Glyn Hughes Hospital,
Belsen
24th November 1945

Feeding is difficult for UNRRA staff. Ration scale DPs, used by British Army—new scale November 1945—did not reduce calorie value—did cause dissatisfaction with patients . . . who were under the impression that they were being given less food because UNRRA had taken over the hospital! Not permitted to give same variety as formerly; now impossible to serve roast beef, meat loaf, etc. because each down—other items added to keep calorie value up viz. 2362 calories per day. Fresh meat two times a week, tinned meat other days. Patients complain not getting enough bread, milk, meat, or [any other] item or diet that they feel is not being given to them. Any complaint investigated—for Tb patients' application has been made to DID Sub Depot for additional food.

Milk not always available—this being investigated. Eggs scarce—none received for six weeks—do have egg powder. Eggs are a necessity for those patients who are suffering from Tb and anaemia, the supply depot [doesn't] have any.

Lack of variety a problem. Reduction in meat allowance—causing problems with cooking good meals.

Reduction in bread allowance 16 oz to 12 oz per person per day another point of dissension. Lack of rolled oats also a problem.

Fresh fruit—always on request. We are not in receipt of any dried fruit, etc. On the whole all patients are receiving an adequate diet, but rather a monotonous one—every effort is at all times being made to vary it as much as possible.

A sample menu is quoted hereunder:

Breakfast
Sausage, bread, butter, jam
Coffee or cocoa

Dinner
Full diet
Beef stew, boiled potatoes, creamed turnips, gravy, bread
Light diet
Milk soup, mashed potatoes, creamed vegs, gravy, bread, milk pudding with raisins

Supper
Bouillon soup with celery and parsley
Fish or cheese or quark
Bread, butter, jam
Coffee or cocoa
Stewed fruits

Special diets as ordered

Doherty Collection, Yad Vashem Archives, Jerusalem, Israel, 0–70/36, volume 3, p. 337.

About the Editors

Judith Cornell AM is a registered nurse with several postgraduate qualifications. She is the former Executive Director of the New South Wales College of Nursing, a position she held for ten years. She has extensive experience as a clinical nurse, teacher and administrator within the health care sector and is a Fellow of the New South Wales College of Nursing. Since retiring in 1996, she has maintained her interest in and commitment to health through her involvement in numerous committees, as a volunteer and as a Director of the South Eastern Sydney Area Health Service Board. Mrs Cornell was made a Member of the Order of Australia in 1995 for her contribution to the quality of nursing practice and education. She is currently undertaking postgraduate studies in Archival Management at Edith Cowan University, Western Australia and continues to research the life and work of Muriel Doherty.

Dr R. Lynette Russell AO is a registered nurse and certified midwife and holds a Diploma of Nursing Education (NSW), Bachelor of Arts (Honours) and a Doctor of Philosophy (Newcastle). She is a Fellow of the New South Wales College of Nursing. She has extensive experience as a clinical nurse and as a nurse educator and academic within the health care and higher education sectors. Dr Russell's research interests centre on the history of nursing and the health care sector, particularly in Australia, and she has a number of publications in this area including *From Nightingale to Now: Nurse Education in Australia*. She is an Emeritus Professor at the University of Sydney following her recent retirement from the position of Foundation Dean, Faculty of Nursing at this university.

Illustration Sources

Page no.

iii Bloch, S. E. (ed.) (1965) *Holocaust and Rebirth: Bergen-Belsen 1945–1965*, Bergen-Belsen Memorial Press, World Federation of Bergen-Belsen Associations, New York, p. 22.

2 Doherty Collection, New South Wales College of Nursing Archives, Sydney, DC/PB148.

10 Doherty Collection, Yad Vashem Archives, Jerusalem, Israel, 0–70/36, volume 2, p. 249a.

15 Doherty Collection, Yad Vashem Archives, Jerusalem, Israel, 0–70/36, volume 1, p. 18.

25 Doherty Collection, Yad Vashem Archives, Jerusalem, Israel, 0–70/36, photograph album, p. 291.

32 Bloch, S. E. (ed.) (1965) *Holocaust and Rebirth: Bergen-Belsen 1945–1965*, Bergen-Belsen Memorial Press, World Federation of Bergen-Belsen Associations, New York, p. 5.

39 Diane Booth, after M. K. Doherty's original sketch in the Doherty Collection, Yad Vashem Archives, Jesusalem, Israel, 0–70/36, volume 1, p. 101.

40 Diane Booth, after M. K. Doherty's original sketch in the Doherty Collection, Yad Vashem Archives, Jerusalem, Israel, 0–70/36, volume 2, p. 62.

41 Diane Booth, after M. K. Doherty's original sketch in the Doherty Collection, Yad Vashem Archives, Jerusalem, Israel, 0–70/36, volume 1, p. 61.

46 Doherty Collection, Yad Vashem Archives, Jerusalem, Israel, 0–70/36, photograph album, p. 286.

52 Bloch, S. E. (ed.) (1965) *Holocaust and Rebirth: Bergen-Belsen 1945–1965*, Bergen-Belsen Memorial Press, World Federation of Bergen-Belsen Associations, New York, p. 66.

61 Bloch, S. E. (ed.) (1965) *Holocaust and Rebirth: Bergen-Belsen 1945–1965*, Bergen-Belsen Memorial Press, World Federation of Bergen-Belsen Associations, New York, p. 73.

70 Bloch, S. E. (ed.) (1965) *Holocaust and Rebirth: Bergen-Belsen*

1945–1965, Bergen-Belsen Memorial Press, World Federation of Bergen-Belsen Associations, New York, p. 77.

73 Doherty Collection, Yad Vashem Archives, Jerusalem, Israel, 0–70/36, photograph album, p. 102.

84 Doherty Collection, Yad Vashem Archives, Jerusalem, Israel, 0–70/36, photograph album, p. 102.

96 Doherty Collection, Yad Vashem Archives, Jerusalem, Israel, 0–70/36, photograph album, p. 209.

110 Doherty Collection, Yad Vashem Archives, Jerusalem, Israel, 0–70/36, photograph album, p. 287.

118 A. M. Rosenblum Jewish Museum, The Great Synagogue, Sydney.

126 Doherty Collection, Yad Vashem Archives, Jerusalem, Israel, 0–70/36, photograph album, p. 84.

142 Doherty Collection, Yad Vashem Archives, Jerusalem, Israel, 0–70/36, photograph album, p. 212.

152 Doherty Collection, Yad Vashem Archives, Jerusalem, Israel, 0–70/36, photograph album, p. 298.

153 Doherty Collection, Yad Vashem Archives, Jerusalem, Israel, 0–70/36, volume 4, p. 523.

164 Doherty Collection, Yad Vashem Archives, Jerusalem, Israel, 0–70/36, photograph album, p. 297.

167 A. M. Rosenblum Jewish Museum, The Great Synagogue, Sydney.

189 Doherty Collection, Yad Vashem Arrchives, Jerusalem, Israel, 0–70/36, volume 4, p. 619.

190 Doherty Collection, Yad Vashem Archives, Jerusalem, Israel, 0–70/36, volume 4, p. 620.

197 Doherty Collection, Yad Vashem Archives, Jerusalem, Israel, 0–70/36, photograph album, p. 211.

204 Doherty Collection, New South Wales College of Nursing Archives, Sydney, DC/P1A

209 Doherty Collection, New South Wales College of Nursing Archives, Sydney, DC/RACP/P115c, P114, P115.

Bibliography

Arad, Y. (ed.) (1994) *The Pictorial History of the Holocaust*, Yad Vashem, Jerusalem, and Macmillan, New York.

Bloch, S. E. (ed.) (1965) *Holocaust and Rebirth: Bergen-Belsen 1945–1965*, Bergen-Belsen Memorial Press, World Federation of Bergen-Belsen Associations, New York.

Colliers Encyclopaedia (1991) Vol. 22, Colliers, Canada, p. 659.

Doherty, M. K. (1945) 'Correspondence to Mother and Friend From Bergen-Belsen', in the Doherty Collection, New South Wales College of Nursing, Sydney.

Doherty, M. K. (1945) 'Letters written when serving at Belsen and in Poland with UNRRA, May–July', Mitchell Library, Sydney, MLMSS 442, Item 6, Box 1(1).

Doherty, M. K. (1996) *The Life and Times of the Royal Prince Alfred Hospital, Sydney, Australia*, edited by R. L. Russell, New South Wales College of Nursing, Sydney.

Doherty, M. K. (1996) *Off the Record: The Life and Times of Muriel Knox Doherty 1896–1988*, edited by R. L. Russell, New South Wales College of Nursing, Sydney.

Doherty, M. K., Sirl, M. B. & Ring, O. I. (1944) *Modern Practical Nursing Procedures*, Dymocks Book Arcade Ltd, Sydney.

Doherty Collection, Yad Vashem Archives, Jerusalem, Israel 0–70/36, photograph album and Vols 1–4 (pp. 1–637).

The New Encyclopaedia Britannica (15th edn), (1994) Vol. 12, Publishing Group, Chicago, p. 150.

UN Information Organisation, (1944) *Helping People to Help Themselves: The Story of the United Nations Relief and Rehabilitation Administration*, published for the United Nations Information Organisation by His Majesty's stationery office, London, p. 3.

UNRRA (1946) *50 Facts About UNRRA*, Division of Public Information, UNRRA, Washington DC, June, p. 1.

INDEX